Arthur Irwin Street

A Chronicle of the War

Arthur Irwin Street

A Chronicle of the War

ISBN/EAN: 9783744685122

Printed in Europe, USA, Canada, Australia, Japan

Cover: Foto ©ninafisch / pixelio.de

More available books at **www.hansebooks.com**

A CHRONICLE

—OF THE—

WAR

Including Historical Documents, Army and Navy Movements, Roster of State Troops, Etc.

——BY——

ARTHUR I. STREET,

Author of "Chronicle of the Panic of 1893," "Handbook of the Venezuelan Question," Etc.

Copyrighted, 1898,

—BY—

ARTHUR L. STREET.

79127

The following compilation is designed to preserve in convenient form a brief resume of the events leading up to, and including the course of, the war between the United States and Spain. It includes all the important dates and documents which the general public are likely to desire to refer to for information or curiosity. The roster of State troops is appended for the advantage of those who may have a personal interest in the army and may desire to follow the movements of friends and relatives.

THE DOCUMENTS.

DE LOME'S LETTER.
FEBRUARY 8, 1898.

The (President's) message has undeceived the insurgents, who expected something else, and has paralyzed the action of Congress, but I consider it bad. Besides the natural and inevitable coarseness with which he repeats all that the press and public opinion of Spain has said of Weyler, it shows once more that McKinley is weak and catering to the rabble, and, besides, a low politician who desires to leave a door open to me and to stand well with the jingoes of his party.

It would be most important that you should agitate the question of commercial relations, even though it be only for effect and that you should send here a man of importance in order that I might use him to make a propaganda among the Senators and others in opposition to the Junta and to win over enemies. (Extracts from letter written by Dupuy De Lome, Spanish Minister to the United States, to Senor Canalejas, editor of El Heraldo, Madrid.)

THE ALLEGED WEYLER LETTER.

"By the way, I have read these days that the Americans are pondering about sending one of their warships to that city. During my command in Cuba they did not even dare to dream about it. They knew the terrible punishment that awaited them.

"I had Havana harbor well prepared for such an emergency. I rapidly finished the work that Martinez Campos abandoned. If the insult is made I hope there will be a Spanish hand to punish it as terribly as it deserves." (Extract from letter alleged to have been written by General Weyler to Santos Guzman. The letter was first given to the press by Honore Laine, a New York newspaper correspondent.)

THE BLOWING UP OF THE MAINE.
FEBRUARY 15, 1898.

WASHINGTON, February 15.—The Secretary of the Navy received the following telegram from Captain Sigsbee:

"Maine blown up in Havana harbor at 9:40 and destroyed. Many wounded and doubtless many killed and drowned. The wounded and others are on board a Spanish man-of-war and the Ward line steamer.

"Send lighthouse tender from Key West for crew and the few pieces of equipment still above water. No one saved other clothes than those upon him.

"Public opinion should be suspended until a further report. All officers believed to be saved. Jenkins and Merritt not yet accounted for.

"Many Spanish officers, including representative of General Blanco, now with me, express sympathy.

"SIGSBEE."

COUSIN'S TRIBUTE.
MARCH 21, 1898.

"The measure now proposed (for the relief of the victims of the Maine disaster) is most appropriate and just, but hardly is mentionable in contemplation of the great calamity to which it appertains. It will be merely an incidental legislative footnote to a page of history that will be open to the eyes of the Republic and of the world for all time to come. No human speech can add anything to the gratitude, the speechless reverence already given by a great nation to its dead defenders and their living kin. No act of Congress providing for their needs can make a restitution for their services. Human nature does in human ways its best, and still is deep in debt. Expressions of condolence have come from every country and from every clime, and every nerve of steel and ocean cable has carried on electric breath the sweetest, tenderest words of sympathy for that gallant crew who manned the Maine." (Extract frem speech in the House of Representatives by Cousins of Iowa, March 21, 1898.)

NOT PREPARING FOR WAR.
FEBRUARY 19, 1898.

WASHINGTON, February 19.—The officials of the War Department are annoyed at the circulation of rumors that seem to connect an activity now observable at the seacoast defenses with the Maine incident. Assistant Secretary of War Meiklejohn declares that the movement has no connection with the Maine affair. There have been increases in the garrisons of the posts, but this has been going on for six months and has only marked a step in the development of the scheme of coast defenses planned by the fortification board some time ago.

Said Mr. Meiklejohn: "It is following out the policy of the department, which has been pursued ever since the ordnance department turned over to the engineers the modern guns which they had manufactured. When these are placed in the coast fortifications it becomes necessary to have them carefully protected, and this work has been going on for six months. Guns have been sent to the Delaware fortifications, Finney Point, Fort Moultrie and other defenses on the Atlantic Coast."

SPANISH REQUESTS REFUSED
MARCH 6, 1898.

WASHINGTON, March 6.—As to the Madrid dispatch regarding the requests of the Spanish Government, the following authorized statement was given out by the State Department.

The President will not consider the recall of General Lee. He has borne himself throughout this crisis with judgment, fidelity and courage, to the President's entire satisfaction.

As to the supplies for the relief of the Cuban people, all arrangements have been made to carry a consignment from Key West by one of the naval vessels, whichever may be most adopted for the purpose, to Matanzas and Sagua La Grande.

AN EMERGENCY APPROPRIATION.
MARCH 7, 1898.

WASHINGTON, March 7.—Chairman Cannon of the Appropriations Committee of the House to-day introduced a bill entitled "Making Appropriations for the National Defense."

That there is hereby appropriated out of any money in the Treasury not otherwise appropriated, for the national defense and for each and every purpose connected therewith, to be expended at the discretion of the President and to remain available until June 30, 1899, fifty million dollars.

"TOGETHER WITH AMERICA."
MARCH 12, 1898.

It has hitherto been the ruling principle in American politics to abstain from alliances with European powers, but the time for alliances has come for the United States. They can no longer afford to view the conflicts of the European powers as something remote and no concern of theirs. It may be a fortunate thing for both that this should be the case, just when it is so very possible for England and the United States to act together. On our side there is every disposition, and we can claim to have shown it in our acts. It is for them to take the next step. They can now, by speaking a word in regard to China, make clear to the world that the two Anglo-Saxon communities are prepared to act together.—St. James Gazette, London, March 12, 1898.

A FINANCIAL VIEW.
MARCH 12, 1898.

LONDON, March 12.—The Statist discusses the financial side of a possible Spanish-American war. After pointing out the expense of hurriedly creating an American army and strengthening the navy, it agrees that the United States would eventually obtain command of the sea, adding: "Then, if Spain submitted, the expenditure would rapidly end and the war might not cost very much. But if

Spain prolonged the contest, the United States would find itself in an embarrassing position. The creation of a large army to drive Spain out of Cuba would mean a very considerable expense, and, when accomplished, what would the United States do with Cuba?. Lastly, if Spain then refused to submit, would America, after capturing the Spanish West Indies, extend the war to Europe? The collapse of Spanish credit might force her to peace; but if Spain, simply defaulting her debt devoted the money she could raise in any way to protection in the struggle, the cost to the United States would certainly be very great."

THURSTON'S CUBAN SPEECH.
MARCH 24, 1898.

"I shall refer to these horrible things no further(the starvation and desolation in Cuba.) They are there. God pity me; I have seen them. They will remain in my mind forever. And this is almost the twentieth century! Christ died 1900 years ago, and Spain is a Christian nation. She has set up more crosses in more lands, beneath more skies, and under them has butchered more people than all the other nations of the earth combined. Europe may tolerate her existence as long as the people of the Old World wish. God grant that before another Christmas morning the last vestige of Spanish tyranny and oppression will have vanished from the Western Hemisphere. I counseled silence and moderation from this floor when the passion of the nation seemed at white heat over the destruction of the Maine, but it seems to me the time for action has now come. Not action in the Maine case. I hope and trust that this Government will take action on the Cuban situation entirely outside of the Maine case. When the Maine's report is received, it if it be found that our ship and sailors were blown up by some outside explosive, we will have ample reparation without quibble or delay; and if the explosion can be traced to Spanish official sources there will be such swift and terrible punishment adjudged as will remain a warning to the world forever. The time for action has then come. No greater reason for it can exist to-morrow than exists to-day. Every hour's delay only adds another chapter to the awful story of misery and death. Only one power can intervene—the United States of America." (Extract from speech of John A. Thurston in the Senate, March 24, 1898.)

THE PRESIDENT'S MESSAGE.
MARCH 28, 1898.

To the Congress of the United States: "For some time prior to the visit of the Maine to Havana harbor our Consular representative pointed out the advantages to follow a visit of national ships to the Cuban waters, in accustoming the residents to the presence of our flag as the symbol of good will and of our ships in the fulfillment of the mission of protection to American interests, even though no immediate need therefore might exist. Accordingly, on the 25th of January last, after a conference with the Spanish Minister in which the renewal of visits of our war vessels to Spanish waters was discussed and accepted, the peninsular authorities at Havana were advised of the purpose of this Government to resume friendly visits at Cuban ports and that with that view the Maine would forthwith call at the port of Havana. This announcement was received by the Spanish Government with appreciation of the friendly character of the visit of the Maine and with the notification of the intention to return the courtesy by sending Spanish ships to the principal ports of the United States.

"Meanwhile the Maine entered the harbor, etc., etc. (The message here reviews the events immediately prior to and including the explosion.)

"The appalling calamity fell upon the people of our country with crushing force and for a brief time an intense excitement prevailed, which in a community less just and self-controlled than ours must have led to hasty acts of blind resentment. This spirit, however, soon gave way to the calmer processes of reason and to the resolve to investigate the facts and await the material proof before forming a judgment as to the cause, the responsibility, and, if the facts warranted, the remedy due. This course necessarily recommended itself from the outset to the Executive, for only in the light of a dispassionately ascertained certainty could it determine the nature and measure of its full duty in the matter.

(The message here reviews the formation of the naval court of inquiry and its findings.)

"I have directed that the findings of the Court of Inquiry and the views of this Government thereon be communicated to the Government of her Majesty, the Queen Regent, and I do not permit myself to doubt that the sense of justice of the Spanish nation will dictate a course of action suggested by honor and the friendly relations of the two governments. It is the duty of the Executive to advise Congress of the result and in the meantime deliberate consideration is invoked.   WILLIAM M'KINLEY.

"Executive Mansion, March 28, 1898."

NAVAL COURT OF INQUIRY.

Captain W. T. Sampson, president of the court; Captain F. P. Chadwick, Lieutenant-Commander Schroeder, Lieutenant-Commander A. A. Marix; Lieutenant-Commander Marix, Judge Advocate.

MAINE INQUIRY REPORT.

KEY WEST, Fla., Monday, March 21, 1898.—After a full and mature consideration of all the testimony before it, the court finds as follows:

First—That the United States battle-ship Maine arrived in the harbor of Havana, Cuba, on the 21st day of January, 1898, and was taken to buoy No. 4, in from five and a half to six fathoms of water, by the regular Government pilot. The United States Consul-General had notified the authorities at that place the previous evening of the intended arrival of the Maine.

Second—The state of discipline on board the Maine was excellent and all orders and regulations in regard to the care and safety of the ship were strictly carried out. All ammunition was stowed away in accordance with instructions, and proper care was taken wherever ammunition was handled. Nothing was stored in any one of the magazines or shell rooms which was not permitted to be stowed there. The magazines and shellrooms were always locked after having been opened; and, after the destruction of the Maine, the keys were found in their proper place in the captain's cabin, everything having been reported secure that evening at 8 P. M. The temperature of the magazines and shellrooms were taken daily and reported. The only magazine which had an undue amount of heat was the after ten-inch magazine, and that did not explode at the time the Maine was destroyed. The torpedo warheads were all stowed in the after part of the ship under the ward room, and neither caused nor participated in the destruction of the Maine. The dry gun-cotton primers and detonators were stowed in the cabin aft and remote from the scene of the explosion. The waste was carefully looked after on board the Maine to obviate danger. Special orders in regard to this had been given by the commanding officer. Varnishes, dryers, alcohol and other combustibles of this nature were stowed on or above the main deck and could not have had anything to do with the destruction of the Maine. The medical stores were stowed after under the ward room and remote from the scene of the explosion. No dangerous stores of any kind were stowed below in any of the other storerooms. The coal bunkers were inspected. Of those bunkers adjoining the forward magazines and shell rooms, four were empty, namely, B3, B4, B5, B6. A15 had been used that date and A16 was full of new river coal. This coal had been carefully inspected before receiving it on board. The bunker in which it was stored was accessible on three sides at all times, and the fourth side at this time, on account of bunkers B4 and B6 being empty. This bunker A16 had been inspected that day by the engineering officer on duty. The fire alarms in the bunkers were in working order and there had never been a case of spontaneous combustion of coal on board the Maine. The two after boilers of the ship were in use at the time of the disaster, but for auxiliary purposes only, with a comparatively low pressure of steam, and being tended by a reliable watch. These boilers could not have caused the explosion of the ship. The forward boilers of the ship have since been found by the divers and are in a fair condition. On the night of the destruction of the Maine everything had been reported secure for the night at 8 P. M. by reliable persons, through proper authorities, to the commanding officer. At the time the Maine was destroyed, the ship was quiet, and, therefore, the least liable to accident caused by movements from those on board.

Third—The destruction of the Maine occurred at 9:40 P. M. on the 15th of February, 1898, in the harbor of Havana, Cuba, being at the same time moored to the very same buoy to which she had been taken upon her arrival. There were two explosions of a distinctly different character, a very short but distinct interval between them, and the forward part of the ship was lifted to a marked degree at the time of the first explosion. The first explosion was more in the nature of a report, like that of a gun, while the second explosion was more open, prolonged, and of a greater volume. This second explosion was, in the opinion of the court, caused by the partial explosion of two or more of the forward magazines of the Maine.

Fourth—The evidence bearing on this, being principally obtained from the divers, did not enable the court to form a definite conclusion as to the condition of the wreck, although it was established that the after part of the ship was practically intact, and sank in that condition a very few minutes after the destruction of the forward part. The following facts in regard to the forward part of the ship are, however, established by the testimony: That portion of the protective deck, which extends from about frame 30 to about frame 41, was blown up aft and over to port. The main deck, from about frame 30 to about frame 41, was blown up aft and slightly over to starboard, folding the forward part of the middle superstructure over and on top of the floor part. This was, in the opinion of the court, caused by the partial explosion of two or more of the forward magazines of the Maine.

Fifth—At frame 15 the outer shell of the ship, from a point eleven and one-half feet from the middle line of the ship and six feet above the keel, has been forced up so as to be about four feet above the surface of the water, therefore about thirty-four feet above where it would be had the ship sunk uninjured. The outside bottom plating is bent into a reversed V shape, the after wing of which, about fifteen feet broad and thirty-two feet in length (from frame 17 to frame 25), is doubled back upon itself against the continuation of the same plating extending forward. From 80 the vertical keel is broken in two, and the flat keel bent into an angle similar to the angle formed by the bottom plating. This break is now about six feet below the surface of the water and about thirty feet above its normal position. In the opinion of the court this effect could have been produced only by the explosion of a mine situated under the bottom of the ship at about frame 18, and somewhat on the port side of the ship.

Sixth—The court finds that the loss of the Maine on the occasion named was not in any respect due to the fault or negligence on the part of any of the officers or members of the crew of said vessel.

Seventh—In the opinion of the court the Maine was destroyed by the explosion of a submarine mine, which caused the partial explosion of two or more of her forward magazines.

Eighth—The court has been unable to obtain evidence fixing the responsibility of the destruction of the Maine upon any person or persons.

W. T. SAMPSON, Captain, U. S. N., President.

A. A. MARIX, Lieut.-Commander, Judge Advocate.

United States Flagship New York, March 22, 1898.

The proceedings and findings of the Court of Inquiry in the above case are approved.

M. SICARD, Rear-Admiral, U. S. N., Commander-in-Chief U. S. naval force of the North Atlantic.

SPAIN'S INQUIRY REPORT.
MARCH 25, 1898.

From declarations made by ocular witnesses and experts the report deduces and proves the absence of all those attendent circumstances which are invariably present on the occasion of the explosion of a torpedo.

The evidence of witnesses comparatively close to the Maine at the moment is to the effect that only one explosion occurred; that no column of water was thrown into the air; that no shock to the side of the nearest vessel was felt, nor on land was any vibration noticed, and that no dead fish were found.

The evidence of the senior pilot of the harbor states that there is abundance of fish in the harbor, and this is corroborated by other witnesses. The assistant engineer of works states that after explosions made during the execution of works in the harbor he has always found dead fish.

The divers were unable to examine the bottom of the Maine, which was buried in the mud, but a careful examination of the sides of the vessel, the rents and breaks of which all point outward, shows without a doubt that the explosion was from the inside.

A minute examination of the bottom of the harbor around the vessel shows absolutely no sign of the action of a torpedo and the fiscal (Judge-Advocate) of the commission can find no precedent for the explosion of the storage magazine of the vessel by a torpedo.

The report makes clear that owing to the special nature of the proceedings and the absolute respect shown for the extraterritoriality of the Maine, the commission has been prevented from making such an examination of the inside of the vessel as would determine even the hypothesis of the internal origin of the accident. This is to be attributed to the regrettable refusal to permit the necessary co-operation of the Spanish commission both with the commander and the crew of the Maine and of the different American officials commissioned to investigate the cause of the accident and, later on, with those employed on salvage work.

The report finishes by stating that an examination of the

inside and outside of the Maine, as soon as such examination may be possible, as also of the bottom where the vessel rests will prove that, supposing the remains of the wreck be not totally or partially altered in the process of extrication, the explosion was undoubtedly due to some interior cause.

MASON FOR WAR.
MARCH 29, 1898.

"Mr. President, I speak only for myself, and I am for war. But gentlemen may say, 'Don't say you are for war—say that you are for armed intervention, which means war.' I believe in calling things by their right names. If we believe that murdering our men, sinking our ships, and lowering our flag is not cause for war, say so, and refer it, as they did the Virginius affair, and allow our brothers to be sold like stock for gold. If it is a cause for war let us assume the responsibility put upon us by the constitution and say so, not only to Spain, but to the whole world. We were in Spanish waters, and over Spanish soil. The harbor is owned and controlled by Spain. The explosives in that harbor were owned and controlled by Spain. If it was a torpedo, it was a Spanish torpedo; if it was a mine, it was a Spanish mine; if it was gun-cotton, it was Spanish gun-cotton, and if it was dynamite, it was Spanish dynamite. The power to explode it was controlled by Spain. A government acts only through its agents. It was owned, located and exploded by Spain, and Spain must answer. Let us awake. Shake off the Chinese narcotic that locks in drowsy indolence murmuring, 'Peace at any price.' Awake as our forefathers did at Concord and Bunker Hill; awake to a glorious war against a nation that burns homes and murders women and children; awake to glorious war that seeks no gain for us in treasure or territory, but a war to drive the oppressor from the continent, to set the Cuban flag in the sky forever, and a war that will help us for generations to come, by giving notice that the honor of our flag and the lives of our citizens must be respected among the nations of the world." (Extract from a speech by Senator Mason in the Senate, March 29, 1898.)

JOINT EUROPEAN NOTE.
APRIL 7, 1898.

The undersigned, representatives of Germany, Austria-Hungary, France, Great Britain, Italy and Russia, duly authorized in that behalf, address in the name of their respective governments a pressing appeal to the feelings of humanity and moderation of the President and of the American people in their existing differences with Spain. They earnestly hope that further negotiations will lead to an agreement which, while securing the maintenance of peace, will afford all necessary guarantees for the re-establishment of order in Cuba.

The powers do not doubt that the humanitarian and purely disinterested character of this representation will be fully recognized and appreciated by the American nation.

THE PRESIDENT'S REPLY.
APRIL 7, 1898.

The Government of the United States recognizes the good will which has prompted the friendly communication of the representatives of Germany, Austria-Hungary, France, Great Britain, Italy and Russia, as set forth in the address of your excellencies, and shares the hope therein expressed that the outcome of the situation in Cuba may be maintenance of peace between the United States and Spain, affording the necessary guarantees for the re-establishment of order in the island, so terminating the chronic condition of disturbance there which so deeply injures the interests and menaces the tranquility of the American nation by the character and consequence of the struggle thus kept at our doors, besides shocking its sentiments of humanity.

The Government of the United States appreciates the humanitarian and disinterested character of the communication now made on behalf of the powers named, and for its part is confident that equal appreciation will be shown for its own earnest and unselfish endeavors to fulfill a duty to humanity by ending a situation the indefinite prolongation of which has become insufferable.

PRESIDENT'S RECOMMENDATIONS.
APRIL 11, 1898.

The grounds for the forcible intervention of the United States as a neutral to stop the war in Cuba may be briefly summarized as follows:

First—In the cause of humanity and to put an end to the barbarities, bloodshed, starvation and horrible miseries now existing there, and which the parties to the conflict are either unable or unwilling to stop or mitigate. It is no answer to say this is all in another country, belonging to another nation, and is, therefore, none of our business. It is expressly our duty, for it is right at our door.

Second—We owe it to our citizens in Cuba to afford them that protection and indemnity for life and property which no government there can or will afford, and to that end terminate the conditions that deprive them of legal protection.

Third—The right to intervene may be justified by the very serious injury to our commerce, trade and business of our people, and by the wanton destruction of property and devastation of the island.

Fourth—And, which is of most importance, the present condition of affairs in Cuba is a constant menace to our peace, and entails upon this Government an enormous expense. With such a conflict waged for years in an island so near us and with which our people have such trade and business relations; when the lives and liberties of our citizens are in constant danger, and their property destroyed and themselves ruined; where our trading vessels are liable to seizure and are seized at our very door by warships of a foreign nation, the expeditions of filibustering that we are powerless to prevent altogether, and the irritating questions and entanglements thus arising—all these, and others that I need not mention, with the resulting strained relations, are a constant menace to our peace and compel us to keep on a semi-war footing with that nation with which we are at peace.—(Extract of special message to Congress from President McKinley, April 11, 1898.)

In view of these facts and these considerations, I ask

Congress to authorize and empower the President to take measures to secure a full termination of hostilities between the Government of Spain and the people of Cuba, and to secure in the island the establishment of a stable government capable of maintaining order and observing its international obligations, insuring peace and tranquility and the security of its citizens as well as our own, and to use the military and naval forces of the United States as may be necessary for these purposes, and in the interest of humanity and to aid in preserving the lives of the starving people of the island, I recommend that the distribution of food and supplies be continued, and that an appropriation be made out of the public Treasury to supplement the charity of our citizens.

The issue is now with Congress. It is a solemn responsibility. I have exhausted every effort to relieve the intolerable condition of affairs which is at our doors. Prepared to execute every obligation imposed upon me by the Constitution and the law, I await your action. (Concluding passage of the President's special message to Congress, April 11, 1898.)

TWO PULPIT UTTERANCES.
(By Cardinal Gibbons.)

This nation is too brave, too strong, too powerful and too just to engage in an unrighteous or precipitate war. Let us remember that the eyes of the world are upon us, whose judgment we cannot despise, and that we will gain more applause and credit for ourselves by calm deliberation and masterly inactivity than by recourse to arms.

(By Rev. Charles H. Parkhurst.)

If the situation is such between Spain and Cuba that we ought as Christians to go to the relief of the Cubans, why, then, let us go. If the words of the Hebrew epistle, " Remember them that are in bonds as bound with them," mean that American Christians ought to fight for oppressed Cubans and murdered Armenians, then let us send an equipped fleet to Havana and dispatch another fleet of the same kind to the Bosporus.

CONGRESSIONAL RESOLUTIONS.
APRIL 18, 1898.

First—That the people of the Island of Cuba are and of right ought to be free and independent.

Second—That it is the duty of the United States to demand that the Government of Spain at once relinquish its authority and government in the Island of Cuba and withdraw its land and naval forces from Cuba and Cuban waters.

Third—That the President of the United States be and he hereby is directed and empowered to use the entire land naval forces of the United States and to call into actual service of the United States the militia of the several States to the extent as may be necessary to carry these resolutions into effect.

Fourth—That the United States hereby disclaims any disposition or intention to exercise sovereignty, jurisdiction or control over said island except for the pacification thereof and asserts its determination when that is accomplished to leave the Government and control of the island to its people.

THE ULTIMATUM.
APRIL 20, 1898.

April 20, 1898.—Woodford, Minister, Madrid: You have been furnished with the text of a joint resolution voted by the Congress of the United States on the 19th inst.—approved to-day—in relation to the pacification of the island of Cuba. In obedience to that act the President directs you to immediately communicate to the Government of Spain said resolution, with the formal demand upon the Government of Spain to at once relinquish its authority in the island of Cuba and withdraw its land and naval forces from Cuba and Cuban waters.

In taking this step the United States hereby disclaims any disposition or intention to exercise sovereignty, jurisdiction or control over the island except for the pacification thereof, and asserts its determination, when that is accomplished, to leave the government and control of the island to its people under such free and independent government as they may establish.

If by the hour of noon on Saturday next, the 23d day of April, there be not communicated to this Government by the Government of Spain a full and satisfactory response to this demand and resolution, whereby the ends of peace in Cuba shall be assured, the President will proceed, without further notice, to use the power and authority enjoined upon him by the said joint resolution to such extent as may be necessary to carry the same into effect. SHERMAN.

WOODFORD DISMISSED.
APRIL 21, 1898.

"In compliance with a painful duty, I have the honor to inform you that there has been sanctioned by the President of the Republic a resolution of both chambers of the United States Congress which denies the legitimate sovereignty of Spain and threatens armed intervention in Cuba, which is equivalent to a declaration of war. The Government of Her Majesty has ordered her Minister to return without loss of time from North American territory, together with all the personnel of the legation.

"By this act the diplomatic relations heretofore existing between the two countries and all of the negotiations between their respective representatives cease.

"I am obliged thus to inform you, so that you may make such arrangements as you think fit. I beg your Excellency to acknowledge receipt of this note at such time as you deem proper. Taking this opportunity to reiterate to you the assurances of my distinguished consideration."

"P. GULLON."

(Note of Spanish foreign Minister to United States Minister Woodford, April 21, 1898.)

BLOCKADE OF CUBA
APRIL 22, 1898.

Whereas, By a joint resolution passed by the Congress and approved April 20, 1898, and communicated to the Government of Spain, it was demanded that said Government at once relinquish its authority and government in the island of Cuba and withdraw its land and naval forces from Cuba and Cuban waters, and the President of the United States was directed and empowered to use the entire land and naval forces of the United States and to call into actual service of the United States the militia of the several States to such an extent as might be necessary to carry said resolution into effect; and whereas, in carrying into effect such resolution the President of the United States deems it necessary to set on foot and maintain a blockade of the north coast of Cuba, including all ports of said coast between Cardenas and Bahia Honda, and the port of Cienfuegos on the south coast of Cuba; now therefore

I, William McKinley, President of the United States, in order to enforce the said resolution, do hereby declare and proclaim that the United States of America has instituted and will maintain a blockade of the north coast of Cuba, including the ports on the said coast between Cardenas and Bahia Honda, and the Port of Cienfuegos on the south coast of Cuba aforesaid, in pursuance of the laws of the United States and the laws of nations applicable to such cases. An efficient force will be posted so as to prevent the entrance and exits of vessels from the ports aforesaid. Any neutral vessel approaching said ports and attempting to leave the same without notice or knowledge of the establishment of such blockade will be duly warned by the commander of the blockading forces, who will indorse on her register the fact and the date of such warning and where such warning was made, and if the same vessel shall again attempt to enter any blockaded port she will be captured and sent to the nearest convenient port for such proceedings against her and her cargo as prize as may be deemed advisable.

Neutral vessels lying in any of the said ports at the time of the establishment of such blockade will be allowed thirty days to issue therefrom.

In witness whereof I have hereunto set my hand and caused the seal of the United States to be affixed.

Done at the city of Washington this 22d day of April,

A. D. 1898, and of the independence of the United States the one hundred and twenty-second.

WILLIAM M'KINLEY.

By the President,
JOHN SHERMAN, Secretary of State.

DECLARATION OF WAR.
APRIL 25, 1898.

Be it enacted: First—That war be and the same is hereby declared to exist, and that war has existed since the 21st day of April, A. D. 1898, including said day, between the United States of America and the Kingdom of Spain.

Second—That the President of the United States be and he hereby is directed and empowered to use the entire land and naval forces of the United States and to call into the actual service of the United States the militia of the several States to such extent as may be necessary to carry this act into effect.

CALL FOR VOLUNTEERS.
APRIL 23, 1898.

Whereas, By an Act of Congress, entitled, "An Act to provide for the increasing of the military establishment of the United States in time of war, and for other purposes," approved April 22, 1898, the President was authorized, in order to raise a volunteer army, to issue his proclamation calling for volunteers to serve in the army of the United States; now, therefore,

I, William McKinley, President of the United States, by virtue of power vested in me by the Constitution and by the laws, and deeming sufficient occasion to exist, have thought it fit to call for and hereby do call for, volunteers to the aggregate number of 125,000, in order to carry into effect the purpose of said resolution, the same to be apportioned as far as practicable among the several States and Territories and the District of Columbia according to population, and to serve for two years unless sooner discharged. The details for this object will be immediately communicated to the proper authorities through the War Department.

In witness whereof I have hereunto set my hand and caused the seal of the United States to be affixed.

Done at Washington this 23d day of April, 1898, and of the independence of the United States the one hundred and twenty-second.   WILLLIAM M'KINLEY.

By the President,
JOHN SHERMAN, Secretary of State.

TO THE NAVAL MILITIA.
APRIL 1, 1898.

The department requests that you will immediately proceed to put the naval militia of your State in thorough condition to meet any sudden call for their services by the President of the United States. The divisions should be recruited to their full strength and thoroughly drilled. A careful inspection should be made of all vessels in the ports of your State that can be utilized for a mosquito fleet in accordance with the instructions and blanks sent to the Adjutant-General. (Letter from the Navy Department to the Governors of all States containing organizations of naval militia, April 1, 1898.)

A CRITIC'S FORECAST.
APRIL 29, 1898.

Spain's most noteworthy point of superiority lies in her torpedo flotilla, but the Spanish boats are nearly all old and, it is feared, in rather bad order. Battleships cannot be improvised or quickly built, while torpedo boats can be adapted or constructed in a short time. Therefore it is worth bearing in mind that in those material elements which it is least easy to create the United States has superiority from the first.

There is more difference in the personnel of the two navies. I do not hesitate to say that the neutral as well as the acquired qualifications of the American naval officers are miles ahead of those of the Spanish. Indeed there is no room for comparison. Moreover, the American naval officers have carefully faced and carefully studied the problems which they are now grappling with, while the Spaniards have shirked the disagreeable subject. Concerning the men, a casual observer is likely to be woefully mistaken. When hard work is to be done the Americans do it with an intelligence and go to which the Spaniards are absolutely strangers. Spain cannot afford to essay an organized or formal attack upon the United States coast.

The Almirante Oquendo might shell Savannah or Wilmington, but it would be foolish to try experiment, which could have no possible influence upon the course of the war. A regular naval bombardment of New York, Boston or Philadelphia is out of the question, because Spain cannot afford to risk her ships against the guns, behind the earthworks or in the water where they could not fail to be torpedoed. The disablement of a Spanish ship off Boston or New York would mean her total loss. Further, Spain cannot permit her fleet to engage in any kind of general action at a point far removed from a coaling station. (Extract from an article by W. Laird Clowes, the British naval critic, on "Some of the Problems of the War." The extract was published April 29, 1898.)

SPAIN'S CONDUCT OF THE WAR.
APRIL 23, 1898.

The Spanish Government considers it indispensable to make absolute reserve on the point of privateering in order to maintain liberty of action and uncontested right to have recourse to privateering when it is considered expedient.

The state of war existing between Spain and the United States annuls the treaty of peace and amity of October 27, 1795, and the protocol of January 12, 1877, and all other agreements, treaties or conventions in force between the two countries.

From the publication of these presents thirty days are granted to all ships of the United States anchored in our harbors to take their departure free of hindrance.

Notwithstanding that Spain has not adhered to the Declaration of Paris the Government, respecting the principles of the laws of nations, proposes to observe and hereby orders to be observed the following regulations of maritime law:

First—Neutral flags cover the enemy's merchandise, except contraband of war.

Second—Neutral merchandise, except contraband of war, is not seizable under the enemy's flag.

Third—A blockade to be obligatory must be effective, viz.: It must be maintained with sufficient force to prevent access to the enemy's littoral.

Fourth—The Spanish Government, upholding its right to grant letters of marque, will at present confine itself to organizing, with the vessels of the mercantile marine, a force of auxiliary cruisers, which will co-operate with the navy according to the needs of the campaign and will be under naval control.

Fifth—In order to capture the enemy's ships and confiscate the enemy's merchandise and contraband of war, under whatever form, the auxiliary cruisers will exercise the right of search on the high seas and in the waters under the enemy's jurisdiction in accordance with international law and the regulations which will be published.

Sixth—Here is explained what is included in contraband of war, naming weapons, ammunition, equipments, engines, and in general all the appliances used in war.

Seventh—To be regarded and adjudged as pirates, with all the rigor of the law, are captains, masters, officers and two-thirds of the crew of vessels which, not being American, shall commit acts of war against Spain, even if provided with letters of marque issued by the United States.

UNITED STATES' CONDUCT OF THE WAR.
APRIL 26, 1898.

This Government will not resort to privateering, but will adhere to the rules of the Declaration of Paris.

First—The neutral flag covers enemy's goods with the exception of contraband of war.

Second—Neutral goods not contraband of war are not liable to confiscation under the enemy's flags.

Third—Blockades in order to be binding must be effective.

Fourth—Spanish vessels in any ports or places within the United States shall be allowed until May 21, 1898, inclusive, for loading their cargoes and departing from such ports or places; and such Spanish merchant vessels, if met at sea by any United States ship, shall be permitted to continue their voyage if on examination of their cargoes it shall be shown that their cargoes were taken on board before the expiration of the above time, provided that nothing herein contained shall apply to Spanish vessels having on board any officers in the military or naval service of the enemy or any coal (except such as may be necessary for their voyage) or any other article prohibited or contraband of war, or any dispatch of or to the Spanish Government.

Fifth—Any Spanish vessel which prior to April 21, 1898, shall have sailed from any foreign port bound for any port or place in the United States shall be permitted to enter such port or place and to discharge her cargo and afterward, forthwith, to depart without molestation, and if met at sea by a United States ship shall be permitted to continue her voyage to any port not blockaded.

Sixth—The right of search is to be exercised with strict regard for the right of neutrals and the voyages of all mail steamers are not to be interfered with except on the clearest grounds of suspicion of a violation of law in respect of contraband or blockade.

THE SHIPS AT MANILA.
MAY 1, 1898.

UNITED STATES FLEET—

Olympia—First class protected cruiser, 5800 tons; speed, 21.69 knots; four 8-inch, ten 5-inch rapid-fire, fourteen 6-pounders, seven 1-pounders, and four machine guns.

Baltimore—Second rate cruiser, 4600 tons; 20.6 knots; four 8-inch, six 6-inch rifles, four 6-pounder rapid-fire, two 3-pounders, two 1-pounders, two 1.8-inch, two 1.4-inch and two machine guns.

Raleigh—Second rate cruiser, 3183 tons; 19 knots; one 6-inch and ten 5-inch rapid-fire rifles, eight 6-pounders, four 1-pounders and two machine guns.

Concord—Third rate cruiser, 1700 tons; 17 knots; six 6-inch, two 6-pounder rapid-fire, two 3-pounders, one 1-pounder and four machine guns.

Petral—Fourth rate, 890 tons; 13 knots; four 6-inch, two 3-pounder rapid-fire, one 1-pounder and four machine guns.

McCulloch—Revenue cutter; four 6-pounders.

Nanchan—Collier.

Zafiro—Supply vessel.

SPANISH FLEET—

Reina Christina—Second rate, 3500 tons; 17 knots; six 6.2-inch Hontoria, two 2.7-inch and three 2.2-inch rapid-fire rifles, six 1.4-inch and two machine guns.

Castilla—Second rate, 3342 tons; 14 knots; four 5.9-inch Krupps, two 4.7-inch, two 3.3-inch, four 2.9-inch, eight rapid-fire and two machine guns.

Velasco—Third rate, 1152 tons; three 5.9-inch Armstrong, two 2.7-inch Hontorias and two machine guns.

Don Antonio de Ulloa and Don Juan de Austria—Third rate, 1130 tons; 14 knots; four 4.7-inch Hontoria, three 2.2-inch rapid-fire, two 1.5-inch and two machine guns.

General Lezo and El Cano—Gun vessels, 524 tons; 11.5 knots; General Lezo—two 4.7-inch Hontorias, one 3.5-inch, two small rapid-fire and one machine gun. El Cano has three 4.7-inch, two small rapid-fire and one machine gun.

Marques del Duoro—Dispatch boat, 500 tons; one smooth bore 6.2-inch, two 4.7-inch smooth bores and one machine gun.

Isle de Cuba and Isla de Luzon—Gunboats, 1030 tons; four 4.7-inch Hontorias, four 6-pounders, two 3-pounders and two machine guns.

Isle de Mindonao—Steamer armed as cruiser, 4195 tons; 13.5 knots.

BATTLE OF MANILA.

MAY 1, 1898.

The American fleet, under Commodore Dewey, entered the bay of Manila at 5 o'clock Sunday morning, May 1, 1898, and anchored at a distance from the Cavite forts. The latter, notwithstanding the long range, opened fire on the Americans and were supported by the Spanish warships which were anchored under the forts.

Commodore Dewey then ordered his squadron to close in and delivered an awful cannonade, using his guns of all calibers for thirty minutes. He then withdrew his vessels beyond the range of the smaller guns and poured shells from his big guns upon the Spaniards, inflicting hideous damage.

The fire lasted for little more than a quarter of an hour. The Spaniards, though greatly weakened, continued to reply. Commodore Dewey, therefore, closed in again and renewed the ceaseless cannonade.

After the fight had continued for an hour the Spanish squadron was practically annihilated and all the forts were silenced. Three of the Spanish ships were on fire, one had sunk and the others were riddled and helpless. The resistance of the Spaniards was admirably stubborn, but they were outmatched. Nevertheless, they did not yield nor did they strike a single flag.

After a lapse of a few hours Commodore Dewey, who had withdrawn to the west side of the bay when the Spanish ceased to fire, returned to Cavite. He was received with some shots from the land forts, whereupon he again opened upon them with a furious torrent of projectiles. In a short time he had silenced them, apparently rendering them totally useless.

The scene during the cannonading was terribly magnificent. The incessant roar of the heavy guns, with the sharper report of quick-firing weapons, combined to make an overpowering, hellish din that was re-echoed from all sides of the land-locked bay.

The maneuvering of the American vessels was constant

and sometimes elaborate. (Extract from a report of the battle printed in the New York Sun May 3, 1898.)

DEWEY'S ORDERS.
APRIL 24, 1898.

WASHINGTON, April 24.—Dewey, Hongkong, China: War has commenced between Spain and the United States. Proceed at once to the Philippine Islands. Commence operations at once, particularly against the Spanish fleet. You must capture vessels or destroy them. Use utmost endeavors. LONG.

DEWEY'S REPORTS.
MAY 1, 1898.

MANILA, May 1.—The squadron arrived at Manila at daybreak this morning. Immediately we engaged the enemy and destroyed the following vessels: Reina Christina, Castilla, Ulloa, Isla de Cuba, General Lezo, Duero, Correo, Velasco, Mindanao, one transport and every battery at Cavite.

The squadron is uninjured, and only a few men were slightly wounded. The only means of telegraphing is to the American Consul at Hongkong. I shall communicate with him. DEWEY.

MAY 4, 1898.

CAVITE, May 4.—Have taken possession of naval station at Cavite, Philippine Islands, and destroyed its fortifications. Have destroyed fortifications at the bay entrance, paroling the garrison. I control the bay completely, and can take the city at any time. The squadron is in excellent health and spirits.

The Spanish loss is not fully known, but is very heavy. One hundred and fifty were killed, including the captain of the Reina Christina. I am assisting the Spanish sick and wounded. Two hundred and fifty sick and wounded are in the hospitals within our lines. There is much excitement at Manila. I will protect foreign residents. DEWEY.

MAY 12, 1898.

HONGKONG, May 12.—There is little change in the situation since my last telegram. I am transferring to transports steel breech-loading rifles from sunken Spanish men-of-war. Also stores from arsenal in my possession. I am maintaining strict blockade. Add Argos to list of destroyed vessels. El Correo probably El Cano.

DEWEY.

MAY 13, 1898.

CAVITE, May 13.—Maintaining strict blockade. Reason to believe that the rebels are hemming in the city by land, but have made no demonstration. Scarcity of provisions in Manila. Probable that the Spanish Governor will be obliged to surrender soon. Can take Manila at any moment. Climate hot and moist. On May 12th captured gunboat Callao attempting to run blockade. Have plenty of coal. One British, one French, two German and one Japanese vessel here observing. DEWEY.

MAY 20, 1898.

MANILA, May 20.—Situation unchanged. Strict blockade continues. Great scarcity of provisions in Manila. Foreign subjects fear an outbreak of the Spanish soldiers, and they will be transferred to Cavite by the foreign men-of-war in the harbor. Aguinaldo, the rebel chief, who was brought here from Hongkong on the McCulloch, is organizing a force of native cavalry, and may render assistance that will be valuable. DEWEY.

THANKS OF THE NATION.
MAY 9, 1898.

Resolved by the Senate and House of Representatives of the United States of America, in Congress assembled, that, in pursuance of the recommendation of the President, the thanks of the Congress and of the American people are hereby tendered to Commodore Dewey, United States Navy, commander-in-chief of the Asiatic squadron, for highly distinguished conduct in conflict with the enemy, as displayed by him in the destruction of the Spanish fleet and batteries in the harbor of Manila, Philippine Islands, on May 1, 1898.

That the thanks of Congress and the American people are hereby extended, through Commodore Dewey, to the officers and men under his command for the gallantry and skill exhibited by them on this occasion.

Be it further resolved, that the President of the United States be requested to cause this resolution to be communicated to Commodore Dewey and through him to the officers and men under his command. (Resolution passed unanimously by both houses of Congress, May 9, 1898.)

THE NEW WORLD'S POWER.
MAY 10, 1898.

Into the putrid swamp of European politics has been cast a stone and the turbid, slimy waters spout up.

The great Republic on yonder side of the ocean, without castles, nobles, or standing army, has suddenly sprung out of her position of neutrality to Europe, and one European State, which has slaughtered myriads of men wrestling for freedom, is undone.

Old Europe in consequence is shaken to her foundations.

It is a new power—no militarism, no huge fleet, yet a mighty, overwhelming, elemental power.

In Asia the same phenomenon has appeared. The new power has become a balance of the scales.

Even if the alliance with England comes to nothing the new American position in the Far East crosses every combination hitherto effected. (Extract from an editorial in the Berlin Social Democratic organ, the Vorwaertz, May 19, 1898.)

MORE VOLUNTEERS.
MAY 25, 1898.

By the President of the United States—a Proclamation.

Whereas, An Act of Congress was approved on the 25th day of April, 1898, entitled, "An Act declaring war exists between the United States of America and the Kingdom of Spain," and

Whereas, By an Act of Congress entitled "An Act for temporarily increasing the military establishment of the United States in time of war and for other purposes," approved April 22, 1898, the President is authorized, in order to raise a volunteer army, to issue his proclamation calling for volunteers to serve in the army of the United States.

Now, therefore, I, William McKinley, President of the United States, by virtue of the power vested in me by the Constitution and the laws, and deeming sufficient occasion to exist, have thought it fit to call forth and hereby do call forth volunteers to the aggregate number of 75,000 in addition to the volunteers called forth by my proclamation of the 25th day of April in the present year; the same to be apportioned, as far as practicable, among the several States and Territories and the District of Columbia, according to population and to serve for two years unless sooner discharged. The proportion of each arm and the details of enlistment and organization will be made known through the War Department.

Done at Washington, May 25, 1898.

WILLIAM M'KINLEY.

RECONCENTRATION REVOKED.
MARCH 30, 1898.

Article 1—After the publication of this order the reconcentrados and their families will be allowed to return home in the provinces of Pinar del Rio, Havana, Matanzas and Santa Clara.

Article 2—Orders all relief committees and military authorities to facilitate the workings of the decree and also to aid the reconcentrados in selecting and securing new houses.

Article 3—Directs the Colonial Government, through its Secretary and Ministerial officers, to prepare to execute all necessary orders to secure for the country people work on public improvements, and also to give food, by economic kitchens, to all the suffering, attention being called to those on the small country estates.

- Article 4—All the expenses over and above the funds now in the hands of the committee are to be provided for under the head of an extraordinary war credit.

Article 5—All former orders of reconcentration are abrogated.

SUNDAY, JANUARY 23.
HAVANA IN POPULAR FERMENT.

Havana streets filled with inflammatory circulars against Americans by ultra-Spanish adherents.

Extra military guard placed about the United States Consular residence.

Passing of eight United States war vessels through Key West causes excitement and apprehension in Havana that vessels have been dispatched to Havana.

Havana Imparcial declares that appearance of war vessels indicates United States desire to seize Cuba.

SUNDAY, JANUARY 24.
THE MAINE ORDERED TO HAVANA.

Battleship Maine ordered to Havana, to resume friendly naval relations with Spain, after abandonment of same by Cleveland administration.

Senators express hope that Maine will be followed by other vessels.

Cipher dispatch received by President McKinley from Consul-General Lee at Havana. President orders direct telegraphic communication with Key West. (Subsequent developments indicated that this telegram was to urge that the Maine should not be sent to Havana.)

TUESDAY, JANUARY 26.
ARRIVAL OF THE MAINE AT HAVANA.

Battleship Maine arrives in Havana harbor; courtesies exchanged with Spanish shore and naval officers.

Madrid newspapers consider visit of Maine inopportune

and encouraging to insurgents. Madrid Imparcial fears visit of Maine will provoke a conflict.

WEDNESDAY, JANUARY 26.
PROVOCATION WITHOUT JUSTIFICATION.

Spanish cruiser Vizcaya ordered to New York to return visit of Maine to Havana.

Madrid Imparcial declares Maine visit a "provocation without justification."

Premier Sagasta not apprehensive of serious consequences because of friendly assurances by President McKinley.

THURSDAY, JANUARY 27.
RUMORS OF IMPENDING FRICTION.

Madrid press allege that battleship Maine was already en route to Havana when Spain was notified of intended visit.

United States Government reported to be making extensive preparations against possible hostile emergency.

Spanish fleet ordered to concentrate at Cadiz.

FRIDAY, JANUARY 28.
RECIPROCITY.

Reciprocity negotiations reported under way with Spain, Cuba and Porto Rico.

SATURDAY, JANUARY 29.
BAD CONDITION OF SPANISH NAVY.

Carlist press in Spain express apprehension at bad condition of Spanish navy.

· Conference between French Minister to Spain and Spanish Minister of Foreign Affairs, presumably with reference to United States. (This was the beginning of an apparent entente, later developing into a reported Franco-Spanish alliance.)

SUNDAY, JANUARY 30.
COURTESIES TO THE MAINE.
Officers of battleship Maine attend bull fight in Havana as guests of Acting Captain-General Parrado.

TUESDAY, FEBRUARY 1.
"MISSION OF PEACE."
Crew of Vizcaya charged by Spanish Admiral with "mission of peace."

TUESDAY, FEBRUARY 7.
MORE TRIAL OF AUTONOMY ASKED
Spain replies to United States note asking for early termination of hostilities in Cuba; reply solicits more prolonged trial of autonomy.

TUESDAY, FEBRUARY 8.
A MINISTER'S LETTER.
Letter of Spanish Minister Dupuy De Lome to Editor Canalejas of Madrid Herald published; letter denounces President McKinley as weak, a caterer to the rabble and a low politician; intimates possible insincerity of Spain in reciprocity negotiations.

HIGH TENSION IN MADRID.
High tension reported in political situation in Madrid.
Madrid El Epoca urges Spaniards to united stand against interference with national honor in Cuba.

SENATE RESOLUTIONS.
Senators Allen, Mason and Cannon introduce resolutions looking toward recognition of Cuban insurgent government.

DE LOME RESIGNS.
Spanish Minister De Lome cables resignation to Madrid.

THURSDAY, FEBRUARY 10.
BEGINNING OF THE END.
Carlist press in Spain declare De Lome letter incident the beginning of the end of Spanish respect for the United States.

SATURDAY, FEBRUARY 12.
DISAVOWAL OF DE LOME.

State Department requests formal disavowal from Spain of De Lome's intimations as to insincerity of Spain in reciprocity negotiations and in autonomy plan in Cuba.

MONDAY, FEBRUARY 14.
A SPANISH FOOL.

Spanish Cabinet Minister states that De Lome letter has resulted in Spanish Cabinet being "placed in false position by a fool."

BERNABE, NEW MINISTER.

Louis Polo y Bernabe selected by Spain as successor to De Lome as Minister to the United States.

TUESDAY, FEBRUARY 15.
BLOWING UP OF THE BATTLESHIP MAINE.

Battleship Maine blown up in Havana harbor by unknown agencies; suspicion attached to Spanish authorities or citizens; 266 men killed, including Lieutenant F. W. Jenkins and Assistant Engineer Merritt.

WEDNESDAY, FEBRUARY 16.
INQUIRIES AND CONDOLENCES.

Formation of naval court of inquiry to investigate cause of destruction of the Maine ordered.

Spanish Charge d'Affaires expresses condolence to President McKinley on Maine destruction.

Flags placed at half mast on Governor-General's palace in Havana in respect to deceased of Maine.

European nations express condolence for disaster.

THURSDAY, FEBRUARY 17.
WARNED OF THE DANGER.

Spanish officer in Havana quoted as saying: "I guess this (Maine disaster) will bring the war that we all wish."

Public funeral in Havana, at General Blanco's request, of victims of Maine disaster.

Secretary Congosto of Cuban Colonial Government

quoted as saying to General Lee: "I warned you that there would be trouble if the Maine came here."

A PATRIOTIC STATE.

Governor Tanner and Legislature of Illinois tender President McKinley financial and moral assistance in case of emergency.

OFFICERS OF INQUIRY COURT.

Naval Court of Inquiry appointed: Captain Sampson, president; Captain Chadwick, Lieutenant-Commanders Schroeder and Marix.

FRIDAY, FEBRUARY 18.
PROTEST AGAINST UNITED STATES DIVERS.

United States divers were not allowed to inspect wreck of Maine unaccompanied by Spanish divers; restriction subsequently withdrawn.

THE SENATE.

Senate tables measure providing for committees to investigate Maine disaster; sharp speeches in debate by Mason, Wolcott and Lodge.

SATURDAY, FEBRUARY 19.
ARMY AND NAVY ACTIVE.

War Department declares that current activities on coast fortifications are not due to Maine disaster.

Orders to Norfolk Navy Yards to hasten work on warships.

Unusual activity reported at many army posts.

SUNDAY, FEBRUARY 20.
VISIT OF THE VIZCAYA.

Spanish cruiser Vizcaya officially received and welcomed in New York harbor; suecial precautions to protect vessel.

MONDAY, FEBRUARY 21.
SPAIN'S CLAIM OF ACCIDENT.

Naval Court of Inquiry convenes on United States steamship Mangrove at Havana.

Premier Sagasta states that inquiry shows Maine disaster was due to accidental internal explosion.

TUESDAY, FEBRUARY 22.
"THE GEORGE WASHINGTON."

Senator Morgan introduces resolution inquiring as to possibility of early construction of a battleship to be named "George Washington" to be equal to any existing warship.

WEDNESDAY, FEBRUARY 23.
NAVY AT KEY WEST.

Battleship Texas sails to Key West to join fleet assembling at that point.

THURSDAY, FEBRUARY 24.
"AMERICAN TREACHERY."

Orders to many post commanders change plans already inaugurated.

Madrid Imparcial urges Spain to prepare for war, because of American treachery.

FRIDAY, FEBRUARY 25.
PURCHASING COAL FOR THE NAVY.

Naval and recruiting stations ordered to hold on waiting lists all applicants for enlistment who have had previous service.

Government said to have purchased 300,000 tons of coal for naval stations in West Indies and on Florida coasts.

PROCTOR INVESTIGATES.

Senator Proctor sails for Cuba to make personal investigation of conditions.

Public feeling reported much excited in Spain over newspaper and popular hostility in United States to Spain.

SATURDAY, FEBRUARY 26.
NOT TO BE JINGOED INTO WAR.

President McKinley quoted as saying that he will not be "jingoed" into war with Spain.

A CHRONICLE OF THE WAR. 39

Assistant Secretary of Navy Roosevelt admits great increase of naval offensive and defensive preparations within past ten days.

Navy Department requests Congress to provide 1500 men for new cruisers.

Five Spanish warships reported to have sailed for the United States.

THE SPANISH POPULACE.

Anti-American feeling increases in Spain; floats ridiculing the United States exhibited in Mardi Gras festivities in spite of police prohibition.

SUNDAY, FEBRUARY 27.

WAR IN APRIL.

Great scarcity of food and bread riots in many provinces of Spain.

Madrid Correspondence Militaire predicts war with the United States by April.

Republican Congressmen restive over delay in Maine and Cuban matters.

Workmen at League Island Navy Yard continue work on Sundays.

MONDAY, FEBRUARY 28.

LIMIT OF CONCESSIONS ON BOTH SIDES.

Reported that President McKinley had indicated March 1st to Spain as limit of time for trial of antonomy; that Spain requested extension of time to May 1st.

Reported that President McKinley demanded recall of Weyler from Captain-Generalship of Cuba, upon alternative of forcible removal by the United States.

Reported that Maine disaster prevents President from carrying out intended Cuban policy.

Madrid Imparcial insists that limit of concessions by Spain to the United States has been reached.

TUESDAY, MARCH 1.

SPANISH HOPE AND CONGRESSIONAL EXAMINATION.

Premier Sagasta expresses hope of favorable Cuban developments by March 1st.

Senators Gallinger, Thurston and Money, and Representatives Cummins and W. A. Smith depart for Cuba on tour of personal investigation of conditions in island.

Ironclad Miantonomoh and Katahdin ordered into commission March 10th; Monitor Amphitrite ordered to join fleet of Admiral Sicard at Key West.

WEDNESDAY, MARCH 2.

SPAIN INVESTIGATES.

General opinion prevails among naval and other authorities that Naval Board of Inquiry will report Maine disaster due to explosion outside of the vessel.

Spain orders appointment of commission to investigate cause of Maine disaster.

Special inducements offered to machinists to enlist in the United States navy.

CAESARISM IN UNITED STATES.

Paris Temps expresses fear of development of Caesarism in the United States.

RELIEF FOR CUBANS.

Cruisers Montgomery and Nashville detailed to transport relief supplies to Cuban reconcentrados in other cities than Havana.

THURSDAY, MARCH 4.

WEYLER ACCUSED.

Wreck of the Maine attributed by press reports to General Weyler, assisted by Senors Trinon, Calvo, Breshes, Vega and Bubir.

Madrid populace much excited over report that United States fleet at Hongkong will proceed against the Philippine Islands.

FRIDAY, MARCH 4.

BUYING WARSHIPS.

President McKinley reported to be considering the purchase of eight warships now building in Europe and offered to the United States.

Navy Department reports construction of proposed warship "George Washington" impracticable.

SECOND SPANISH FLEET.

Second Spanish naval and torpedo squadron reported fitting out at Cadiz for expedition to Cuba.

DEWEY'S FLEET.

Preparations made to replenish supplies of United States fleet at Hongkong.

WHEAT.

Wheat exports threaten exhaustion of available United States supply.

SATURDAY, MARCH 5.

OTHER NATIONS WANT WARSHIPS.

Navy Department experiences difficulty in securing recruits for new vessels.

Lieutenant Kelley reported to be conducting general inspection of available auxiliary naval vessels.

Work begun on refitting of old monitors in League Island Navy Yard.

Navy Department contracts for delivery of 400,000 tons of coal at Key West.

Lively competition in bidding for foreign war vessels expected between the United States, Spain and other nations.

Navy Department reported to have plans for emergency completion of 100 torpedo boats within ninety days.

United States reported to have secured plans of Spanish harbors and defenses.

BRITISH SYMPATHY.

British sympathy reported to support United States against Spain.

Spanish agents in negotiating for war vessels in England allege British sympathy with Spain; British Government issues contradiction.

French foreign office reported to be urging mediation between United States and Spain.

SPANISH REQUESTS REFUSED.

Spain advertises pardon to deserters and fugitives from military service.

Spain requests withdrawal of Consul-General Lee; United States refuses request.

Spain requests that relief supplies for Cuba be sent in merchant marine instead of in war vessels; United States refuses request.

SUNDAY, MARCH 7.

FIFTY MILLIONS FOR NATIONAL DEFENSE.

Representative Cannon introduces a bill appropriating $50,000,000 for national defense, to be expended at the discretion of the President and to be available until June 30, 1899.

Spain withdraws request for recall of Consul-General Lee.

Dispatch boat Fern ordered to replace Montgomery and Nashville in distribution of supplies to Cubans; change of vessel approved by Spanish press as friendly.

Numerous agents of foreign ship-building yards call upon President McKinley with reference to sale of war vessels.

Commander W. H. Brownson departs for Europe to investigate foreign war vessels available for purchase.

Orders issued for enlisting of two additional regiments of artillery. (This was in accordance with a special bill passed by Congress.)

STOCK EXCHANGES DEMORALIZED.

London and New York markets demoralized by scare at Spanish-American situation. Paris bourse affected for the first time by Spanish-American affairs.

FRENCH SYMPATHY.

Press reports allege French sympathy with Spain, due

to French desire to check growing commercial and financial power of United States.

TUESDAY, MARCH 8.
NOTABLE WAR SPEECHES.

Cannon bill appropriating $50,000,000 for national defense unanimously passed by the House of Representatives amid great enthusiasm.

Notable speeches in support of measure by Cannon, Henderson, Dollliver, Bailey and Sayres, all speeches deprecating possibility of war and considering appropriation a guarantee of peace.

WAR EXCEPT IN NAME.

Represetative Mann considers that war exists except in name.

Feeling reported in Washington official circles that situation with Spain is much improved.

Many conferences between war and navy officials.

AVAILABLE MUNITIONS OF WAR.

Manufacturing firms in all sections consulted as to capacity for furnishing arms to the Government.

Six nations reported to be bidding for Chilean warships.

WEDNESDAY, MARCH 9.
MATERIAL FOR EMERGENCY.

Senate passes Cannon $50,000,000 appropriation unanimously.

President McKinley signs Cannon appropriation bill.

Reported that Cannon appropriation will be applied first to purchase of additional warships.

Ordnance manufacturers and army and navy supply merchants assure the Government of ability to furnish material for emergency.

Cruiser Montgomery arrives in Havana harbor.

THURSDAY, MARCH 10.
EXPECTATIONS OF PEACE.

Feeling prevails in official and financial circles that difficulties with Spain will be adjusted peaceably.

Monitor Miantonomoh and ram Katahdin go into commission.

Conference of navy officers on arming of auxiliary navy; present crews of auxiliary vessels to be enlisted.

PORTO RICO.

Official advices declare success of autonomy in Porto Rico.

FRIDAY, MARCH 11.

NEW WAR DEPARTMNT.

Military department of the Gulf established, headquarters at Atlanta, Ga., in lieu of department of Texas; General Graham in command.

General Flagler, Chief of Ordnance Department given full power to purchase munitions of war.

RETIRED NAVAL OFFICERS SUMMONED.

Numerous retired naval officers ordered to hold themselves in readiness for service.

Orders issued for manning new fortifications on Atlantic Coast.

Newly organized Sixth Regiment of Artillery stationed at Fort Slocum, N. Y.; Seventh Regiment stationed at Fort Henry, Md.

Battery of Fourth Artillery ordered to Sheridan Point, Va., to defend capital.

Captain Peral, president of the Spanish Court of Inquiry, holds theory of Maine explosion by torpedo untenable.

Spanish Minister Bernabe officially received at Washington.

TRADE NOT AFFECTED.

Weekly trade reports show no decrease in trade activities due to political situation.

SATURDAY, MARCH 12.

NEW INVENTIONS.

Battleship Oregon ordered to cruise south from San Francisco toward Valparaiso.

Special board appointed to consider vessels offered for

auxiliary navy; Lieutenant Kelley advisory member of board.

Many new inventions of war appliances, etc., offered to the War Department.

War Department decides to open bids for projectiles without awaiting appropriation.

Completion of big guns in manufacture at Washington Navy Yard hastened.

British press apprehend war between United States and Spain.

SUNDAY, MARCH 13.
FORECAST OF SPANISH ACTIONS.

Reported that Spanish Board of Inquiry will conclude Maine disaster due to internal causes.

Madrid press state that Spain will leave provocation of war to United States.

Warships Helena and Bancroft ordered home from Europe.

Madrid press urge privateering as best method of warfare.

MONDAY, MARCH 14.
NAVY, GUNS, PROJECTILES AND EXPENSES.

Auxiliary navy inspection board organizes, with Captain Frederick Rogers as chairman; American line steamships St. Louis and New York and other vessels inspected.

Bids requested for disappearing gun carriages.

Bids opened for armor-piercing projectiles and 12,-000,000 rifle ball cartridges.

Estimate of $491,131 as cost for maintenance of new artillery regiments submitted.

SPANISH NAVY MOVES.

Spanish naval squadron reported to have left Cadiz, presumably for Porto Rico.

AUSTRIA.

Reported that Austria is urging European powers to join in protest against war between United States and Spain.

British Government refuses to reply to interrogations as to negotiations looking to naval support of the United States.

A SPANISH CHALLENGE.

Senator Mason challenged to duel by editor of Spanish newspaper El Cardo.

Navy purchases Brazilian cruisers Amazonas and Abruall.

TUESDAY, MARCH 15.
PARTY FAILURE PREFERRED TO UNHOLY WAR.

President McKinley quoted as saying: "I would rather my administration should be an ignominious failure than that it should be responsible for an unholy war."

Senate committee decides to postpone investigation of Maine disaster.

Consul-General Osborne speaks in London on advantage of British-American co-operation.

TH ETRIP OF THE OREGON.

Battleship Oregon ordered to join Sicard's fleet at Key West; Captain Charles E. Clark placed in command.

Reported that one Spanish naval squadron will proceed to Havana; second squadron to Porto Rico.

WEDNESDAY, MARCH 16.
SPAIN'S DISPLEASURE AT NAVAL ACTIVITIES.

Spain intimates displeasure at United States naval and military activities, and concentration of fleet at Key West; considers same an encouragement of Cuban insurgents.

Gathering of naval vessels at Key West becomes largest since Civil War.

Five million dollars from emergency appropriation asked for Atlantic and Gulf fortifications, and $2,225,000 for arms and ammunition.

PATRIOTISM FOR POLITICAL EFFECT.

Spirited debate in House of Representatives on Cuban situation; administration accused of arousing patriotic impulses of nation for political effect.

THURSDAY, MARCH 17.
PROCTOR REPORTS.

Senator Proctor reports to the Senate his observations in Cuba; states that reports of suffering of reconcentrados have not been overdrawn; that it is too late for autonomy to succeed.

ARMY REORGANIZATION.

Representative Hull introduces bill prepared by War Department for placing army on war footing with full strength of 104,000 men. (This bill was passed subsequently.)

Reported that President has been advised of findings of Maine Board of Inquiry, for personal guidance; special precautions taken to prevent premature publication of report.

SECOND NAVAL SQUADRON.

Orders issued for formation of additional naval squadron at Hampton Roads.

First disbursement of Cannon appropriation is made for rapid-fire guns purchased in England.

Honore Laine, press correspondent, publishes alleged letter of General Weyler intimating preparations for injury to United States war vessels upon arrival in Havana harbor.

Spanish naval squadron ordered not to proceed to Havana.

FRIDAY, MARCH 18.
GALLINGER ON CUBA.

Brazilian cruiser Amazonas formally transferred to the United States, with assurances of Brazilian friendship.

Senator Gallinger, returning from Cuba, declares that condition of reconcentrados has not been overdrawn.

Efforts made to purchase torpedo boat destroyers in Europe, in accordance with decision of naval strategy board that such craft are necessary.

Contracts awarded for large orders of armor and deck piercing projectiles.

GREAT BRITAIN DON'T WANT HAWAII.

Official denial made in Parliament that Great Britain has planned or desires absorption of Hawaiian Islands.

SATURDAY, MARCH 19.

EUROPEAN COALITION AGAINST UNITED STATES.

All classes of Great Britain and majority of British press alleged to be enthusiastic supporters of the policy of the United States toward Spain.

Spanish newspaper, El Globo, ridicules the United States navy.

Same paper re-asserts that Emperor William of Germany has declared that the United States will not be allowed to wrest Cuba from Spain.

Same paper predicts European coalition against the United States.

Large numbers of cavalry horses purchased in the Black Hills, South Dakota.

Naval Bureau of Ordnance contracts for 4,500,000 pounds of brown powder.

Contract let for dredging of Dry Tortugas harbor, to permit closer anchorage.

MEDIATION SOUGHT.

Reported that Spain is endeavoring through Austria to secure mediation of European powers with United States.

Battleship Oregon sails for San Francisco.

UPRISING IN PORTO-RICO.

Reported that insurrection is imminent in Porto Rico and that Spanish cruiser Vizcaya has been dispatched to port to maintain order.

SUNDAY, MARCH 20.

THE PRESIDENT TAKES CONTROL.

President McKinley reported to be in close touch with all United States representatives abroad; representatives report personally to the President.

Cabinet holds a Sunday meeting.

Continued warlike preparations at army posts, especially at coast points.

Regiment of volunteer heavy artillery of previous war service raised at Waterville, Me., and tendered to the President.

"STAR-SPANGLED BANNER."

Audience at benefit in New York to sufferers of Maine disaster rise and sing "The Star-Spangled Banner."

HASTENING RECIPROCITY.

Reported that Spain has ordered additional concession, including extension to Philippines to hasten reciprocity negotiations with the United States.

SPANISH CENSORSHIP.

More strict censorship of news of Spanish naval movements is ordered.

MONDAY, MARCH 21.

TO PREVENT CONGRESSIONAL EXCITEMENT.

Press forecast of report of Maine Board of Inquiry state that board will attribute explosion to outside causes, but will not fix responsibility for same.

Steps taken by supporters of administration to prevent excitable outburst of Congress upon receipt of Maine inquiry report.

PRESIDENTIAL POLICY.

Congressmen, after conference with members of the Cabinet, predict that President McKinley will recommend interference in Cuba.

NO INDEMNITY FOR THE MAINE.

Reported that Spain will not consider possible demands for indemnity for destruction of the Maine.

THE FLYING SQUADRON.

Announced that flying squadron will be formed at Hampton Roads, presumably under Commodore Howell.

Brazilian cruiser Amazonas rechristened the New Orleans; Abruall rechristened the Albany.

Artillery expert Captain William P. Duvall ordered to

Washington to confer on plans for Atlantic and Gulf coast defenses.

Navy Department advertises for recruits; contracts for extra supplies of pork and beef.

Castle Island in Boston harbor closed to the public.

Two resolutions looking to intervention in Cuba introduced into the House of Representatives.

COUSIN'S TRIBUTE TO THE MAINE.

Notable speech in the House of Representatives by Cousin of Iowa commemorative of the victims of the Maine.

TUESDAY, MARCH 22.
INTERVENTION IN CUBA IS FORESHADOWED.

Lieutenant-Commander Marix departs from Key West for Washington with the findings of the Maine Board of Inquiry.

General opinion in Washington foreshadows United States intervention in Cuba.

UNITED STATES DEFEATS AUTONOMY.

Madrid Imparcial declares that United States action has practically defeated autonomy.

COALING STATION.

Navy Department considers acquiring of coaling station in the West Indies.

WEDNESDAY, MARCH 23.
CONCENTRATING NAVAL MOVEMENTS.

Arrangements made for transfer of revenue cutter service to the Navy Department.

Three warships recalled from foreign waters.

Eight old monitors ordered into condition for protection of New York, Boston and Philadelphia.

Monitors Terror and Puritan ordered to Key West.

Naval strategic board decides to concentrate vessels on the Atlantic Coast.

Dry Tortugas transferred to Navy Department and bids opened for extensive improvements.

Bids opened for extensive improvements at Key West.

A CRISIS APPROACHING.

President continues full and frank conferences with party leaders in Congress. General feeling in Washington that situation with Spain is reaching a crisis.

Senator Bacon introduces resolution in behalf of maintaining peace so long as consistent with national dignity and honor.

Senator Galllinger speaks in Senate on personal observations of situation in Cuba.

Additional pro-Cuban resolutions introduced into the House.

FAMINE SUFFERERS.

Consul Barker reports 50,000 people suffering from famine in Santiago de Cuba province; Consul McGarr reports 15,000 sufferers in district of Cienfuegos.

Naval medical board reports in favor of retirement of Admiral Sicard for physical disability.

STOCK MARKETS DOWN.

All stock markets of the world depressed by the Spanisth-American situation.

THURSDAY, MARCH 24.

SITUATION CRITICAL.

Situation consideration in Washington to be grave and critical, more threatening than at any time since Maine disaster.

Remarkable activity in Navy and War Departments in hastening war preparations.

MAINE REPORT.

Report of the Maine Board of Inquiry delivered to President McKinley and Secretary Long.

JOINT WAR BOARD.

Arrangements made for joint war commission of War and Navy Departments.

Democrats comply with wishes of President McKinley looking to temperate control of Congress on receipt of Maine inquiry report.

THURSTON'S SPEECH FOR CUBAN INDEPENDENCE.

Senator Thurston, at request of his late wife, who died during his visit to Cuba, delivers impassioned speech on Cuban horrors and favoring immediate intervention in behalf of independence.

Vice-President does not check applause in galleries at the close of Thurston's speech.

SPAIN'S TORPEDO FLOTILLA.

Reported that Spanish torpedo flotilla has started westward; that United States has protested that the presence in Cuban waters of warships not directly serviceable against the insurgents will be considered an act of hostility; Spanish Minister confers with State Department with reference to this matter.

NAVAL COMMANDERS.

Numerous assignments of naval commanders; Admiral Sicard retired on leave of absence; Captain Sampson appointed commander of fleet at Key West, the Atlantic squadron; Captain Robley D. ("Fighting Bob") Evans made commander of the battleship Iowa.

Navy Department purchases eight steam yachts and four steam tugs.

NAVAL RESERVES.

Reported that Massachusetts and New York naval militia have been ordered to man monitors in New York and Boston harbors.

FRIDAY, MARCH 25.
SPAIN NOTIFIED OF MAINE INQUIRY REPORT.

Spain notified that Maine Board of Inquiry finds the disaster due to explosion outside the ship.

Spain notifies United States that Spanish Board of Inquiry finds Maine disaster due to explosion inside the ship.

Two extended Cabinet meetings held to consider the Maine inquiry report.

Expected that President McKinley will transmit Maine inquiry report to Congress on March 28th, together with request for relief appropriation for Cuban reconcentrados.

UNPRECEDENTED WAR PREPARATIONS.

War preparations continue on unprecedented scale; country said to be practically on a war footing. Reported that Spain holds the armament of Dry Tortugas more hostile than the dispatch of the torpedo flotilla to Cuba.

Flying squadron definitely formed at Hampton Roads, with Commodore Schley in command.

A DULL LEAD COLOR.

Orders issued to paint all warships a dull lead color.

President McKinley declines to accept movement of Spanish torpedo flotilla as a hostile act.

Recruiting officers at all points ordered to secure as many experienced seamen as possible.

SATURDAY, MARCH 26.

PRESIDENT AND CONGRESS CO-OPERATE.

Hourly consultations between the President and leading members of Congress; general official restlessness reported.

Congressional leaders agree to refer President's message and Maine inquiry report to committees without debate.

Numerous cablegrams pass between the United States and Spanish Governments.

Assistant Secretary of State Adee assigned to preparation of diplomatic correspondence, etc.

Preparations made for transfer of lighthouse tenders to Navy Department to serve as part of coast patrol.

Lieutenant-Colonel A. W. Wagner designated to act with Captain A. S. Barker on joint navy and army commission.

WAR AS SPANISH SALVATION.

Press reports state that Sagasta Ministry begins to look upon war with United States as only means of escaping bankruptcy, by repudiating national indebtedness.

French Government interpellated as to Spanish-American situation; accused of indifference to aggressions of Anglo-Saxon on Latin race. Premier Hanotaux replies that France is friendly to both nations and will act in behalf of peace.

LAST HOPES OF PEACE.

Premier Sagasta expresses belief that means still exist for avoiding a rupture with the United States.

Embassador White receives assurances that Emperor William made no pro-Spanish utterances.

SUNDAY, MARCH 27.
SPAIN CRIES, "NO SURRENDER."

Press gives advance summary of report of Maine Board of Inquiry.

Motto of "No Surrender" reported to prevail among all classes of Spain; Government receives offers of support of men and money from all provinces.

European powers reported friendly to Spain because of danger of overthrow of monarchy in event of war.

SPANISH PATRIOTISM.

Many Spanish citizens volunteer to contribute one day's wages toward purchase of a warship.

Duke of Veragua expresses lack of confidence in President McKinley; considers latter proud and vain.

UNITED STATES HYPOCRISY.

Madrid press declares that Spain will not relinquish Cuba and that United States hypocritically desires possession of the island.

Spain requests further delay of action in regard to Cuba in order to submit further plan for liberal government of the island.

President McKinley reported unwilling to accept any scheme Spain may propose.

THE PURCHASE OF CUBAN INDEPENDENCE.

Reported that commission of financiers have visited Washington to offer to loan Cuban insurgents $200,000,000 with which to purchase independence.

Senator Hanna and other advocates of peace policy reported to be changing attitude on prospect of Spanish increase of martial strength to point of ability to defy the United States.

Secretary Gage reported to be endeavoring to effect peaceable settlement; favors plan of purchase of Cuban independence.

AN ULTIMATUM.

Reported that President McKinley has cabled notes to Spain during the week demanding cessation of war in Cuba and informing Spain of findings of Maine Board of Inquiry.

Reported that Spain has replied that invasion of Spanish rights in Cuba will not be tolerated.

EUROPE EXPECTS EARLY WAR.

European press think that United States has reached limit of extension of time for termination of Cuban hostilities and that Spain has reached limit of concessions; early conflict expected.

German press apprehensive for the first time of belligerent developments.

MONDAY, MARCH 28.
MAINE INQUIRY REPORT IN CONGRESS.

President McKinley transmits findings of the Maine Board of Inquiry to Congress.

Report exonerates officers and crew of the Maine from responsibility and finds that disaster was due to explosion of submarine mine, but fails to fix responsibility for the explosion.

President's accompanying message states that substance of report has been conveyed to the Spanish Government, leaving the question of reparation open to the voluntary determination of Spain.

Report and message referred to committees in both houses without delay.

A HAVANA PLOT.

Report includes testimony of the overhearing of conversation indicating plot of Havana citizens to blow up the Maine.

VOLUNTEER RESERVE.

National Volunteer Reserve formed under command of Lieutenant-General Schofield, retired, and aided by many retired army and navy officers; all living Generals of North and South to be members of military committee; governors of States asked to assist.

Admirals of United States and British fleets at Hongkong reported to have had conference.

INTERVENTION VS. RECOGNITION.

Talk of consolidation of members of House of Representatives favorable to immediate intervention in Cuba.

Representatives of both houses of Congress inform President McKinley of indisposition to delay action in Cuban matters.

Motion made for continuous session of Senate Committee until Maine, Cuban and Spanish questions are settled.

MOSQUITO FLEET.

Reported that "mosquito fleet" will be formed consisting of yachts, tugs, etc., for mobile defense of seacoast.

ARMISTICE.

Foreign press favors granting of armistice between Spanish forces and insurgents in Cuba until fall, pending negotiations between Spain, Cuban insurgents and the United States for adjustment of pending difficulties.

Paris Temps, presumably under inspiration of Premier Hanotaux, urges arbitration to settle the Spanish-American dispute.

TUESDAY, MARCH 29.

ALIGNMENT OF CONGRESSIONAL FORCES.

Reported that unless negotiations now pending with Spain result in adjustment of Cuban question (within ten days) entire diplomatic correspondence will be submitted to Congress and diplomatic negotiations be suspended.

Reported that Spain has offered to grant armistice with Cubans.

Opposition to pacific and conservative policy of President McKinley becomes very strong in both houses; meeting of members of lower house opposed to delay held, under chairmanship of Hopkins of Illinois.

Populists and Silver Republicans in caucus authorize resolutions for immediate recognition of Cuban insurgents.

LESS APPREHENSIVE.

Extreme energy of War and Navy Department in preparations for war relaxed.

Spanish press, public and bourse reported less apprehensive of war.

Twenty-fifth Infantry (colored) transferred from Montana to Dry Tortugas to become acclimated for possible service in Cuba.

Numerous resolutions looking to recognition of Cuban independence introduced into both branches of Congress.

Several resolutions declare war with Spain.

MASON'S IMPASSIONED SPEECH.

Senator Mason delivers impassioned speech on President's message declaring in favor of immediate war; speech is loudly applauded by the galleries.

WEDNESDAY, MARCH 30.

ORDER OF RECONCENTRATION REVOKED.

Captain-General Blanco announces that pacification of eastern provinces of Cuba has progressed so far that order concentrating population in cities will be withdrawn and reconcentrados will be allowed to return to their homes.

Profound excitement reported in House of Representatives on presentation of resolution by Bailey recognizing Cuban independence.

REPUBLICAN BOLT AVERTED.

Republicans are with difficulty prevented from supporting the resolution; resolution laid on the table.

Republicans immediately express to the President hope that something will be done in Cuban matter. President reported to have given assurance that something definite can be expected by April 1st.

SPAIN RELIEVES THE RECONCENTRADOS.

Reported that Spain had addressed a note to the European powers on the situation with the United States and that Premier Hanotaux's declaration on March 26th was due to this note.

Spain said to be considering the granting of an armistice.

Spanish Cabinet votes 3,000,000 pesetas to relief of Cuban reconcentrados.

Spanish financial papers point out disastrous consequences of war.

ISLAND OF ST. THOMAS.

Negotiations reported under way for purchase of the Danish West Indies island of St. Thomas as coaling station for United States navy.

Additional resolutions looking to Cuban independence and resolutions declaring war with Spain introduced into the House.

PRESIDENT NOT UNDULY PRESSED.

Caucus of House Republicans decide to allow President to complete pending negotiations with Spain before taking action.

Senate committee postpones action pending completion of current negotiations with Spain.

THURSDAY MARCH 31.
SPAIN REPLIES TO ULTIMATUM.

Spanish reply to demands of President McKinley are received; reported to declare that Spain cannot admit interference with integrity of empire.

Spain telegraphs United States demand and Spanish reply to all European powers.

Senator Hanna present with President and some members of Cabinet on receipt of Spain's reply.

SENATE FOR RECOGNITION.

Senate committee reported to have concluded informally in favor of immediate intervention in behalf of Cuban independence.

Captain-General Blanco issues decree allowing return of all reconcentrados to their estates and extending aid to the impoverished.

Blanco transmits report to legation in the United States setting forth improved condition of reconcentrados, etc., in Cuba.

GROSVENOR DEFENDS THE ADMINISTRATION.

Impression of Republicans of House after visiting the President is that the latter is not confident of preserving peace.

Representative Lewis condemns alleged negotiations looking to the purchase of Cuban independence.

Representative Grosvenor states that no such negotiations are pending; Grosvenor charges Bailey with making party capital out of the Cuban question.

Rates on war risks in marine insurance advance 50 per cent over preceding day.

Army and Navy Departments begin to give attention to planning campaign.

STRENGTH OF THE MILITIA.

Statement issued showing total number of men in United States available for military duty, 10,378,118.

Statement issued showing authorized strength of State militia to be 186,848, with actual strength of 113,760.

Woodwork removed from all warships at Key West and latter placed in readiness to move at fifteen minutes' notice.

Naval strategic board decides to order all State naval militia to be got in readiness for service.

FRIDAY, APRIL 1.
CUBA MUST ASK FOR ARMISTICE.

Cabinet considers Spain's reply unsatisfactory.

Reply emphasizes repeal of reconcentrado order in Cuba, assents to United States assistance in relief work, consents to armistice, provided Cubans apply for same, but leaves adjustment of hostilities in Cuba to the Colonial Parliament which does not meet until May 4th.

ARBITRATION OF MAINE DISASTER.

Reply suggests that responsibility for Maine disaster be left to the determination of an international board.

Reported that Pope Leo is endeavoring to prevail upon both Spain and Cuban insurgents to accept armistice.

MAINE DESTRUCTION A CAUSE FOR WAR.

Reported that Senate Foreign Committe will report on

Monday, April 4th, the Foraker resolution favoring armed intervention in Cuba, holding revocation of reconcentrado order as a subterfuge, destruction of Maine as sufficient cause for war, and damage to American interests in Cuba as justification for intervention.

CUBANS WANT NO ARMISTICE.

Announced that General Gomez on behalf of insurgents will accept armistice only when sought by Spain under flag of truce.

Cuban Colonial Government makes formal appeal to President McKinley against intervention, on ground that Colonial Government represents majority of people of Cuba.

THREE NEW BATTLESHIPS.

House of Representatives passes naval appropriation bill, including appropriation for three new battleships; many warlike speeches made favoring substitution of action for diplomacy; debate as to utility of modern battleships; galleries crowded and demonstrative.

Reported that Spanish Queen Regent has made personal appeal to Queen Victoria to co-operate with France and Austria in intervention; Queen Victoria refers the appeal to Salisbury.

Governors of States not having naval militia requested to form same.

SEIZURE OF HAWAIIAN ISLANDS.

Reported that instructions have been issued to Admiral Miller to raise United States flag on Hawaiian Islands in event of war with Spain.

STATE APPROPRIATIONS.

New York and Ohio Legislatures appropriate $1,000,000 for contingent war fund; Iowa Legislature appropriates $500,000.

Bill for purchase of British West Indies temporarily withdrawn to avoid creating opposition to President.

END OF DIPLOMACY.

New York and London stock markets believe that end of diplomatic negotiations has been reached.

SATURDAY, APRIL 2.
A WAR MESSAGE.

President McKinley begins preparation of message to Congress; consults with Congressmen and officials of War and Navy Departments; message expected in Congress by Wednesday or Thursday of ensuing week.

SPAIN'S SHIPS STOP AT CAPE VERDE.

Spanish torpedo flotilla puts in at St. Vincent, Cape Verde Islands.

Spanish Cabinet reported divided on reply to United States.

Panic on Madrid bourse.

Reported that European powers are urging Spain to grant an armistice.

Many military and naval preparations ordered in Spain.

CATHOLIC MEDIATION.

Reported that Cardinal Gibbons and Archbishop Ireland are in Washington to urge avoidance of hostilities between United States and Spain.

WAR REVENUE.

Secretary Gage and Representative Dingley confer with President on formulating of war revenue bill.

CARLISTS.

Reported that Spanish royal family fears uprising of Carlists.

SUNDAY, APRIL 3.
CUBAN INDEPENDENCE NOT ASKED.

Republican leaders in Congress endeavor to restrain radical members from breach with President on Cuban matter; bolt of 25 Republicans would give Democratic policy of immediate intervention free play.

Premier Sagasta states that the United States has not asked Spain to grant independent government to Cuba.

Spanish press resumes belligerent tone.

PRIVATEERING.

National subscription for strengthening of Spanish naval fleet announced; all classes of people of Spain, including Carlists, offer their services in event of war. Spanish merchants and sea captains apply for letters of marque to fit out as privateers.

MONDAY, APRIL 4.
PAPAL EFFORTS FOR PEACE.

Spain accepts offer of Pope to use influence with Cuban insurgents upon condition of Spain suspending hostilities.

Spain announces that Pope, at request of President McKinley, has intervened in existing dispute.

State Department denies that President McKinley has requested or accepted Papal mediation.

AMERICANS IN CUBA AND HAVANA.

Americans in Havana become panic-stricken over disturbed popular conditions in the city; Consul-General Lee requests ships for transporting Americans from the city; United States steamships Bache and Blake assigned for the purpose.

Many Cuban families hurry from the island.

Announced that naval auxiliary inspection board has purchased ten auxiliary cruisers.

Washington Post states that war will ensue unless Spain within forty-eight hours grants demands of the United States.

DECLARATION OF PARIS.

Question of obligation of the United States to the terms of the declaration of Paris as to privateering raised in the British Parliament.

DEMOCRATS.

Representative Bailey states that Democrats will not delay action for further negotiations with the "butchers of Spain."

TUESDAY, APRIL 5.
REMOVAL OF AMERICANS FROM CUBA.

Much correspondence had between State Department and Consul-General Lee as to removal of Americans from Cuba; Lee states that Americans cannot be removed in less than five days.

All consuls in Cuba ordered to be ready to concentrate

in Havana and Matanzas; six naval vessels ordered to Cuba to assist in transporting consuls and Americans residents.

Many Senators declare determination to oppose any action short of recognition of Cuban independence; conference of Senators Hanna, Platt of Connecticut, Spooner, Hale, Fairbanks and Aldrich looking to upholding of probable recommendation of President for intervention without recognition.

Reported that Senate Foreign Committee will not report Cuban resolutions until time has been allowed for removal of Americans and consuls from Cuba.

Many conferences, presumably on Spanish-American situation, between delegations of Great Britain, France, Italy and Austria at Washington.

EUROPEAN INTERVENTION.

Reported that movement for European intervention was inaugurated by Spain, urged by Emperor of Austria because of relationship to Queen Regent, urged by France because of financial interest in Spanish bonds, not heartily accepted by Germany because of popular opposition; non-concurred in by Great Britain; latter's attitude probably checks movement.

Sharp speech arraigning Spain made by Turpie of Foreign Relations Committee of the Senate.

CHICKAMAUGA.

Troops at Fort Sheridan, Illinois, ordered south; infantry at Cheyenne, Salt Lake and Fort Leavenworth ordered into readiness to move; troops in south to be concentrated at Chickamauga.

EXCHANGES GIVE UP.

Sanguine expectations in Spanish-American situation disappear from New York stock exchange.

WEDNESDAY, APRIL 6.
WAR MESSAGE WITHHELD.

President McKinley withholds message from Congress until Monday, April 11th, on telegram from Consul-General Lee that Americans cannot be removed from the island before that date. (Statement was made subsequent that the message was withheld in response to request of the Pope in expectation of a successful move toward ensuing peace.)

House committee invited to the State Department to inspect telegram from Lee.

Democrats consent to withhold action until Monday.

Reported that European financial and diplomatic agents have influenced President to withhold message.

Legations of Great Britain, Germany, France, Austria and Italy meet in Washington to frame joint note to United States with reference to Spanish-American difficulties.

Much activity manifested by advocates of intervention and of independence in both branches of Congress, especially in the lower house.

CUBANS AGAINST INTERVENTION.

Counsel of Cuban Junta announces that Cuban insurgents will not accept intervention without recognition.

THURSDAY, APRIL 7.
JOINT EUROPEAN NOTE.

Embassadors of Great Britain, Germany, France, Austria, Italy and Russia present joint notes to United States and Spain hoping for maintenance of peace; note construed by the press to be indorsement of United States policy, because of unwillingness of Great Britain to accept any other attitude.

SPANISH DETERMINATION.

Spanish Foreign Minister Gullon declares that Spain has reached limit of concessions.

Much public anxiety in Madrid over the situation.

Extraordinary sessions of Cabinet decide upon abiding by previous determinations.

Pope renews confidential representations to Spain at midnight; Cabinet declines same as being too late.

PEACE PARTY OF WALL STREET.

Consul-General Lee ordered to withdraw from Havana on April 9th.

Sharp debate in the House over delay of action on

Cuban matter; Lentz charges President McKinley with acting in interest of "peace party" of Wall street; Grosvenor replies that war with Spain is inevitable unless Spain changes attitude.

COAL TRUST.

Senator Morgan asserts that coal trust has been formed to control coal supply of the United States in event of war.

Reported that Spain has bought Welsh coal at 45 shillings per ton, high price being due to strike in Wales coal mines.

Reported that fifteen Spanish war vessels are to be dispatched to the Cape Verde Islands.

Many captains and officers of Spanish merchant marine offer services to the Government.

FRIDAY, APRIL 8.

CUBAN JUNTA IN CONGRESS.

Congressmen, with few exceptions, anticipate early war with Spain.

Numerous members of Cuban Junta appear before Senate and House committees to give information as to condition and needs of insurgents.

Orders issued to naval officers to report at once to vessels.

Reported that Spanish Minister has not called at State Department during past seven days.

Joint meeting of steering committees of both houses of Congress endeavors to secure reversal of committee report for intervention and recognition.

BANKERS TAKE ACTION.

J. Pierpont Morgan and New York bankers confer on Spanish-American situation; emissary of meeting reported to have proceeded to Washington to confer with administration.

AMERICANS LEAVE PORTO RICO.

Consul Hanna and American colony withdraw from San Juan de Porto Rico to St. Thomas Island because of hostility of populace.

TRADE CHECKED.

Trade reports indicate check to new business in Eastern sections because of political situation.

SATURDAY, APRIL 9.

HOSTILITIES IN CUBA SUSPENDED.

Spain yields to solicitation of European powers and grants suspension of hostilities in Cuba; ministers of war and marine reported as objecting.

Reported that 20,000 troops are to leave Spain for Porto Rico; that second naval squadron is to be formed at Cadiz.

Reported that Great Britain did not participate in urging armistice; France took lead.

LEE LEAVES HAVANA.

Consul-General Lee and many Americans withdraw from Havana on the United States steamship Fern; consulate left in charge of British Consul Gollan.

Consuls in Spain give permission to withdraw if considered necessary.

Photographers barred from navy yards; persons observed taking notes are placed under arrest.

BOUNTY FOR SEAMEN.

Bounty of $300 to $500 offered for seamen.

Michigan Legislature appropriates $500,000 for war contingency.

WAR AGAINST ANGLO-SAXON RACE.

London Spectator declares that coalition of European powers against the Monroe doctrine would involve war against Anglo-Saxon race, Great Britain co-operating with the United States.

Reported that naval attaches have been instructed to cease negotiations abroad for further war vessels.

Reported that foreign policy of Queen Regent has been directed from the Vatican at Rome.

ACCUMULATING MONEY.

Deposits of New York associated banks decrease $12,399,900 during current week; loans decrease $8,067,900.

SUNDAY, APRIL 10.
UNITED STATES' GOOD FAITH IN CUBA NOT CREDITED.

Minister Bernabe presents notice of suspension of hostilities in Cuba to the State Department.

Two meetings of Cabinet held to consider the suspension and possible changes in President's message.

Carlist and Republican papers, and upholders of Robledo and Weyler, oppose the suspension of hostilities.

Reported that Congressmen in face of responsibility are becoming less belligerent; Democrats insist upon recognition of Cuban insurgents.

Press on continent of Europe reported unwilling to believe in United States' good faith in Cuban intervention.

Disorderly crowds parade Madrid streets making patriotic demonstrations.

MONDAY, APRIL 11.
PRESIDENT'S MESSAGE TRANSMITTED.

President McKinley transmits message to Congress reviewing negotiations with Spain with reference to terminating hostilities in Cuba and to the destruction of the battleship Maine in Havana harbor. Outline of message is as follows:

President submitted proposal to Spain on March 27th for an armistice with Cubans until October 1st with a view to adjustment of peace.

President at same time insisted upon immediate revocation of the order of reconcentration in Cuba.

END OF NEGOTIATIONS.

Spain replied on March 31st offering to confide arrangement of peace with Cuban insurgents to the Cuban Colonial Parliament; also agreeing to armistice if same were proposed by the insurgents.

President terminated negotiations upon receipt of this reply.

President holds that insurgent government cannot be

GROUNDS FOR CUBAN INTERVENTION.

President recommends armed intervention in Cuba to restore order, upon grounds of (1) humanity; (2) protection to American life and property; (3) injury of hostilities to commerce; (4) menace of hostilities to United States peace; (5) vast expense to the United States in preventing filibustering.

SPAIN RESPONSIBLE FOR THE MAINE.

President holds that destruction of Maine was outcome of Spanish inability to maintain order; states that Spain has proposed to submit question of cause and responsibility of Maine destruction to board of international experts, but that President has made no reply to this offer.

President asks for Congressional authority to intervene to restore order in Cuba and to establish a stable government.

SUSPENSION OF HOSTILITIES TOO LATE.

President announces that Spain has ordered suspension of hostilities in Cuba since the suspension of negotiations on part of President.

CONSULAR REPORTS.

Consular reports setting forth conditions in Cuba transmitted with the message to Congress; reports indicate extreme destitution of reconcentrados throughout the island.

House and Senate refer both message and consular reports to committees without debate.

Galleries of both houses crowded during reading of the message; no demonstration during reading or at close.

FORAKER'S STRUGGLES FOR CUBAN INDEPENDENCE.

Senator Foraker of Foreign Committee reported to be extreme and determined in struggle for recognition as well as intervention.

Stormy meeting of House committee reported during consideration of message.

Democrats of House Foreign Committee and Senators White, Gorman and Teller meet to consider Cuban action; Democrats reported disposed to make the Cuban recogni-

Continued public demonstration in Madrid.

BEEF FOR THE ARMY.

Reported that Government has secured option on sufficient Western cattle to feed army of 100,000 men for twelve months; action taken to defeat syndicate attempting to corner market.

LEE'S WELCOME.

Consul-General Lee welcomed by public demonstrations on passage through Georgia.

———◆———

TUESDAY, APRIL 12.

LENTZ'S ATTACK ON THE PRESIDENT.

Many resolutions in both houses of Congress looking both to mere intervention and to recognition.

Representative Lentz attacks vacillation of President McKinley and arraigns alleged "midnight conferences" with Senator Elkins and John J. McCook, who are alleged to represent interest of Cuban bondholders.

Representative Grosvenor states that President intended by his message to request authority to establish independence in Cuba.

POPULAR PRESSURE FOR WAR IN SPAIN.

Press reports indicate crisis impending in Spain, with civil war imminent if the Cabinet does not yield to popular pressure for war; Cabinet divided in sentiment, Moret leading peace party and Gullon leading war party.

Statement of Navy Department shows vessels now building to range in percentage of completion from $35\frac{1}{2}$ to 94.

GOMEZ TO JOIN THE ATTACK ON HAVANA.

Reported that General Gomez is preparing for land attack on Havana in conjunction with naval attack by the United States.

First battalion of New York naval reserves departs for League Island.

Reported that President has endeavored to dissuade Consul-Genelal Lee from giving full testimony before Senate committee.

LEE ACCUSES SPANISH OFFICERS.

Lee testifies before Senate committee that the Maine was

undoubtedly blown up by agency of Spanish officers, without sanction or knowledge of General Blanco.

Republican members of Ways and Means Committee of the House agree upon plan for raising war revenue by extra taxation of wine, beer, luxuries, etc.; also upon issue of war loan of $500,000,000.

WEDNESDAY, APRIL 13.
HOUSE FOR INTERVENTION.

House of Representatives, by vote of 322 to 19, passes resolution directing President to immediately intervene in Cuba to stop the war, restore peace and establish free and independent government.

SENATE FOR INDEPENDENCE.

Senate foreign committee reports resolution declaring that people of Cuba are and of right ought to be free, demanding that Spain relinquish authority in Cuba, and directing the President to enforce this demand.

Report of Senate committee, prepared by Davis, sharply arraigns Spanish failure to maintain order in Cuba and holds same responsible for the destruction of the Maine.

Minority of House committee report resolution recognizing the Republic of Cuba, directing the President to intervene in aid of the Republic, and authorizing immediate relief to the famine sufferers.

ANNIVERSARY OF FORT SUMPTER.

Day in the House is full of exciting incidents; fact recalled that day is the anniversary of the firing on Fort Sumpter at the beginning of the Civil War; galleries crowded in both houses; populace besieging the Capitol for admission at daybreak.

Motion looking to recognition of Cuban independence defeated in the House by vote of 190 to 146.

LIABILITY FOR CUBAN BONDS.

Sharp debate had in the Senate on liability of the United States for Cuban bonds in event of intervention.

Senate asks State Department for all diplomatic correspondence with Spain and for statement as to whether Cuban independence has been demanded of Spain.

Democrats of House and Senate remain in close touch on Cuban action.

SPANISH CONCESSIONS FOLLOWED BY AMERICAN AGGRESSION.

Official note in Madrid states that Cabinet has decided not to recede from determination to maintain integrity of Spanish territory.

Spanish press expresses impatience at policy of concessions "always followed by further American aggressions."

Spanish press consider that Cuban insurrection would have been suppressed long since save for American interference and assistance.

Proclamation of suspension of hostilities by General Blanco reported to be vague and incapable of execution.

Spain gives order to English firm to supply all possible munitions of war until May 1st.

General conviction prevails in New York stock exchange that Congressional resolutions will lead to war.

SPANIARDS SELL JEWELS FOR WAR FUNDS.

Spanish Cortes summoned to meet six days in advance of regular opening date.

Entire Spanish press believes war inevitable.

Leading Spanish families send jewels to London for sale in order to raise contributions for the national war fund.

Queen Regent heads national subscription with donation of 1,000,000 pesetas.

THE PARALLEL OF TEXAS AND HAWAII.

Senate galleries crowded and thousands of people eager to hear speeches on Cuban resolutions turned away.

Senator Hoar compliments Davis for ability manifested in preparation of report of foreign committee accompanying resolutions.

Numerous speeches for and against Cuban resolutions; Turpie cites parallel of recognition of Texan independence when State contained only 800 inhabitants and of Hawaii when republic was only twenty-four hours old.

European powers begin exchange of notes with view to intervention.

British press considers war inevitable; Chronicle suggests alliance of United States and Great Britain to effect freedom of Cuba by overwhelming display of force; same paper alleges common interest of United States and Great Britain in China.

NEWS OF NAVY MOVEMENTS STOPPED.

Navy Department prohibits anouncements of movements of warships.

Bids opened for transportation of troops from Atlantic and Gulf ports to Cuba.

One thousand mules ordered purchased for transportation purposes.

VOLUNTEERS AND BUSINESS OCCUPATIONS.

John Wanamaker assures employes volunteering for war of reinstatement at close of war and of other emoluments during service or in event of death. American Express Company makes similar offer.

(Similar offers and guarantees made in all parts of the United States and in all lines of occupation during succeeding weeks.)

Madrid press print inflammatory articles against the existing dynasty. Numerous Carlists and notorious revolutionists arrested.

POPE PRAYS TO AVERT BLOODSHED.

Pope Leo states after mass that he has prayed with fervor for averting war; desires to see his pontificate terminated without bloodshed; prays to be removed from earth that he may not behold bloodshed.

TESTIMONY OF LEE AND SIGSBEE.

Testimony of Consul Lee and Captain Sigsbee before Senate foreign committee published; Lee states belief that Maine explosion was due to agents of General Weyler; says Maine explosion was celebrated in various revelries by Spanish officers; asserts that Cuban insurgents have only a skeleton of a government with 31,000 to 32,000 armed men; that Spain has force of 55,000 to 56,000 in Cuba.

Captain Sigsbee testifies that submarine mine causing explosion must have been too large to admit of being planted at night during presence of the Maine in Havana harbor.

THE WORD "INDEPENDENT" NOT USED.

Reported that dispatches of President to Minister Woodford used word "stable" in place of "independent" in demand upon Spain; that word "independent" was intended but was not used by Minister Woodford in negotiations.

FRIDAY, APRIL 15.
CUBAN RECOGNITION A PRESIDENTIAL FUNCTION.

Nine speeches in the Senate for and against Cuban recognition.

Senator Wolcott expresses apprehension of syndicates and commercialism taking advantage of chaotic state of government in Cuba.

Reported that President McKinley will approve the Congressional resolutions whether declaring for mere intervention or for recognition, but that he will decline to act upon instructions for recognition, claiming latter to be entirely the function of the President.

ARMY CONCENTRATED IN THE SOUTH.

Orders issued for concentration in the South of six cavalry regiments, twenty-two infantry regiments and five light batteries of artillery; movements to be made as soon as possible; probable destination, Cuba; Major-General J. S. Brooke to command at Chickamauga.

LEE AND VOLUNTEERS.

Reported that Consul-General Lee will be appointed Major-General of volunteers, to lead troops in Cuban invasion.

Reported that President will call for 50,00 volunteers.

Spanish pretender Don Carlos declares his loyalty to existing order; will proceed against Government only if policy of humiliation is pursued.

GOOD TARGET WORK OF FLYING SQUADRON.

Navy Department decides to charter American line steamers Paris, New York, St. Louis and St. Paul; commanders assigned.

Naval militia in New York, Maryland, Massachusetts, Michigan and New Jersey ordered to be ready to man auxiliary navy.

Newly acquired torpedo boat Somers puts in at English port because of leakage; crews refuse to proceed.

Preliminary trial of flying squadron off coast results in satisfactory target practice, excellent utility of rapid-fire guns and practical service ability of automatic loaders.

SATURDAY, APRIL 16.

SENATE VOTES FOR INDEPENDENCE.

Senate, by a vote of 67 to 21, adopts resolution recognizing the Cuban Republic, requiring Spanish withdrawal from the island, and United States interference to enforce both declarations.

Senator White, in strong speech, opposes any action whatever looking to intervention in Cuba.

Senator Elkins declares that Cuba, Porto Rico and the Philippines should be seized to secure indemnity for the war.

Senator Thurston supports resolution, notwithstanding protest of Republicans on ground that resolution was of Democratic origination.

INFLUENCE OF WILLIAM J. BRYAN.

Only two Democrats oppose recognition; 19 Republicans oppose; Democratic unanimity ascribed by Republicans to visit to Washington and activities of William J. Bryan, former Democratic candidate for President.

Resolutions as adopted contain amendment by Teller disavowing intention of United States to declare sovereignty or jurisdiction over Cuba.

RESIGNATION OF ROOSEVELT.

Reported that Assistant Secretary of the Navy, Theodore Roosevelt, has tendered resignation in order to enter volunteer army service.

Mob attacks United States Consulate at Malaga, Spain;

SUNDAY, APRIL 17.
FEAR OF SAFETY OF THE OREGON.

Committee of Cuban Colonial Parliament sets out to treat with insurgents as to suspension of hostilities and adjustment of terms of peace.

Apprehension expressed that Spanish torpedo gunboat Temerario, in port at Buenos Ayres, will attempt to disable the United States battleship Oregon, en route from San Francisco.

Bill prepared in War Department giving President authority to call out 100,000 volunteers; protests of numerous companies of State militia against service under other than State officers causes change of department plans with reference to calling out the militia.

DISTINGUISHED VOLUNTEERS.

General Lew Wallace withdraws from candidacy for the United States Senatorship from Indiana and tenders war services to the President. (Numerous prominent citizens in all parts of the United States, in the days immediately succeeding, offered personal services, equipments of regiments, yachts, money, etc., to the President for the same purpose.)

LEE FOR PRESIDENT.

Reported that Tammany Hall, Cook county Democracy of Illinois and Duckworth Club of Cincinnati are planning nomination of General Fitzhugh Lee for President on Democratic ticket in 1900.

MONDAY, APRIL 18.
CUBANS ARE AND OF RIGHT OUGHT TO BE FREE.

House and Senate after numerous conferences adopt compromise resolutions declaring that the Cuban people "are and of right ought to be" free and independent; demanding withdrawal of Spain from Cuba; directing President to carry resolutions into effect; disavowing intention of United States to exercise sovereignty or jurisdiction in Cuba.

Conference committee of House contends against adopting words "are and" in resolutions.

Populists unanimously support the Senate resolution.

PRESS DISPATCH BOAT.

Former filibustering vessel Dauntless released on bonds to act as dispatch boat of the Associated Press.

President Frank Thompson of Pennsylvania Railroad Company summoned to Washington to act as special aid to Secretary of War in arranging army transportation.

INDIAN OUTBREAKS.

Many requests made upon department for troops to guard against possible Indian outbreaks following withdrawal of regular army posts. (Numerous assignments were made for this purpose during subsequent days.)

Sick leave of Admiral Sicard revoked, and Sicard ordered to duty at office of Secretary of Navy.

VESSELS RE-NAMED.

Auxiliary cruisers New York and Paris renamed Harvard and Yale respectively. (For rechristening of other vessels of auxiliary navy see tabulated statements under head of Auxiliary Navy.)

POPULAR DISORDER IN SPAIN.

Renewed popular disturbances at Valencia and elsewhere in Spain. (Valencia is headquarters of large number of Carlists.)

COAL IS CONTRABAND.

British order that coal be considered contraband of war reported to be in compliance with desire of United States, to cripple operations of Spanish navy in the West Indies.

Supply of coal for Spanish navy at Cape Verde reported short.

Sales of stocks on New York exchange decline almost to smallest total recorded.

TUESDAY, APRIL 19.

VOLUNTEERS TO BE CALLED OUT.

Text of Congressional resolutions cabled to Minister Woodford.

Reported that President has drafted note to Spain demanding answer not later than Saturday of current week as to United States demand for withdrawal from Cuba.

Stated that owing to constitutional prohibition preventing State militia from service outside of the United States, the President will call for volunteers, giving the State militia the first opportunities of enlistment.

FOREIGN VOLUNTEERS.

Many British people apply at United States legation in England for enlistment as volunteers. (Volunteers were numerous subsequently in many portions of the world, including Greece, Australia and South Africa; numerous British officers sought commissions in the volunteer service.)

Infantry, cavalry and artillery begin movement from many posts to concentration in the South; popular demonstration given in honor of departing troops at all points through which troops pass.

"REMEMBER THE MAINE."

Cry of "Remember the Maine" greets troops at all points. (This cry subsequently became universal in connection with army movements, naval battles, popular demonstrations. It was heard in the battle of Manila at the beginning of Dewey's attack.)

SPAIN IN MEXICO.

Texas "Rangers" ordered to concentrate on Mexican frontier to repel possible invisions from Mexico. (Subsequent information stated that Spanish agents were engaged in endeavoring to foster raids by Mexican frontiersmen.)

EXORBITANT PRICES.

Many tenders of war vessels made to Navy Department at exorbitant prices; attempts also were made to extort unreasonable charges for supplies and munitions of war. (Considerable official and popular indignation was felt at this action.)

Majority of naval officers on detached or shore duty apply to be restored to sea service.

CUBAN GRATITUDE.

Cuban Junta issues statement expressing gratitude for the Congressional resolutions.

RESTRICTION OF THE WAR TO THE WEST INDIES.

Reported that European powers are moving to have Spanish-American war confined to the West Indies. (Subsequent authentic information stated that three European powers, presumably Austria, France and Germany, approached Great Britain with a view to co-operation to this end, but Great Britain peremptorily declined and the action was allowed to lapse.)

Resolutions of inquiry introduced into Congress as to fate of 300 Americans left in Matanzas by Consul Brice upon latter's withdrawal.

BRITISH SUPPORT OF MONROE DOCTRINE.

Sir Frederick Pollock of Oxford University publishes letter advocating British co-operation with the United States in support of the Monroe dictrine. (Public utterances in Great Britain in behalf of united Anglo-American action were very numerous subsequently, culminating in the open declaration by Secretary Chamberlain early in May.)

A CALAMITY.

Government supporters in both branches of the Spanish Cortes meet and ratify attitude of Premier Sagasta; latter declares that charge of responsibility for the Maine disaster to Spain is calumnious.

Spanish Republican party appeals to Castelar to join the parliamentary campaign.

BILLS OF ARMY INCREASE.

Bills for increase of military establishment of the United States introduced into both branches of Congress; bills provide for enlistment of the State militia as volunteers; bills provide for increase of regular army only while war exists or is impending.

WEDNESDAY, APRIL 20.
THE LAST DEMAND.

President McKinley transmits ultimatum to Spain as previously outlined; copy of ultimatum is delivered to Spanish Minister Bernabe.

BERNABE'S PASSPORTS.

Spanish Minister Bernabe demands and is given his passports.

Spanish Cortes opens; Queen Regent reads speech from the throne; blames United States for violation of peaceful attitude; declares against concessions of United States demands, and calls for popular support of throne of her son.

SPAIN WILL NOT ACCEDE.

Republican minority agrees to support necessary war measures.

"Strange and touching seriousness" reported to be overhanging the Cortes proceedings.

House of Representatives, without division, passes bill authorizing President McKinley to call for volunteers.

SPAIN'S NAVAL PLANS.

Reported that Spanish navy plans scattered attacks on comparatively undefended United States ports.

More than 1000 physicians apply to the Surgeon-General of the army for appointment as volunteers.

Governor Atkinson of Georgia announces that he will lead the Georgia militia. (Numerous other State Governors or officials made similar announcements subsequently.)

Affairs of Spanish legation at Washington consigned to care of Austrian and French legations. (Owing to protest of United States against dual representation, Austria and France subsequently agreed upon formal division of jurisdiction of Spanish interests.)

Bill introduced in Congress exempting from annual mining assessment all miners volunteering for war service. (This bill was passed and approved.)

THE MYSTERY OF THE CAPE VERDE FLEET.

Reported that Spanish fleet has sailed west from Cape Verde. (Numerous conflicting reports as to the sailing and destination of this fleet were published during subsequent weeks; both official and press circles were baffled as to its whereabouts until it was finally and definitely reported off the Island of Martinique in the French Indies.)

BREAD RIOTS AND GRAIN DUTIES.

Much anxiety reported felt in Europe over possible short grain supply owing to Spanish-American war. (The price of wheat advanced subsequently to high levels—as indicated in table appended herewith—causing bread riots in several European countries and the suspension of imposts on grain imports in Spain, France, Italy and Austria.)

THURSDAY, APRIL 21.
PASSPORTS TO WOODFORD.

Spain issues passports to United States Minister Woodford, prior to delivery by latter of ultimatum from President McKinley; note accompanying the passports states that Spain considers the Congressional resolutions equivalent to a declaration of war.

DIPLOMACY WITHOUT A CIPHER.

Reported (with many verifications) that ultimatum of President McKinley, transmitted to Minister Woodford in English, instead of in the customary diplomatic cipher, was withheld over night by the Spanish Cabinet and considered by them.

RESPONSIBLITY FOR BREACH OF PEACE.

President's ultimatum allows Spain until noon of Saturday, April 23d, for reply.

Official statement issued that further diplomatic relations with Spain are unnecessary, and placing responsibility for breach of peace upon Spain.

BLOCKADE OF CUBA.

Atlantic squadron of the navy, under Rear-Admiral Sampson, ordered to proceed at once to blockade the northern and a portion of the southern coast of Cuba; squadron ordered to capture or destroy all Spanish vessels.

Atlantic squadron departs from Key West at 2:30 A. M.

WOODFORD AND CONSULS LEAVE SPAIN.

Minister Woodford instructs Consul-General Bowne at Barcelona to order withdrawal of all consuls in Spanish territory.

Affairs of United States legation at Madrid consigned to the British legation.

Minister Woodford withdraws from Spain, accompanied by staff of legation. (During subsequent passage through Spain of train bearing Woodford and staff the Spanish populace frequently assaulted the conveyances.)

THE SITUATION IN SPAIN.

Spanish Foreign Minister declares in the Cortes that relations with the United States have been terminated.

Marshal Campos makes patriotic speech in Cortes, declaring that integrity of Spanish territory will be maintained.

Spanish naval squadron at Cape Verde Islands reported to be awaiting orders, with fires banked.

Call for 80,000 Spanish reserves authorized.

National subscription in behalf of Spain opened in Paris. (Similar subscriptions were opened in many countries subsequently; they were stopped in Great Britain; efforts to check them nearly precipitated internal dissension in Uruguay.)

THE PHILIPPINES.

Orders reported cabled to Commodore Dewey to embark from Hongkong with fleet, presumably for demonstration before Manila in the Philippines.

Expected that full naval program will be put in operation not later than Sunday, April 24th.

Arrangement made in War Department for calling out of 100,000 volunteers.

NO PRIVATEERING.

Announced in British Parliament that the United States has given notice of intention to observe the terms of the Declaration of Paris in regard to vessels of neutral powers, during the war with Spain.

TREASURY CONDITION.

Cash balance on hand in the United States Treasury, $220,479,165; gold reserve, $180,015,560.

Resolutions introduced into House of Representatives for coinage of bullion in Treasury and for issue of legal tender notes to provide war revenue.

Captain-General Blanco issues call to Cubans and Spaniards to unite in defense of the island.

Resignation of Postmaster-General Gary; appointment of Charles Emory Smith of Philadelphia as successor to Gary.

Cargo of 1200 mules and horses on vessel Catalina bound for Spanish army in Cuba seized at New Orleans.

Senate and House pass resolutions giving President power to prohibit export of coal and munitions of war.

GREAT BRITAIN AND THE EUROPEAN POWERS

Paris Temps asks if Great Britain intends to disassociate itself from European powers and co-operate with the United States.

Henry White, secretary of the United States legation to Great Britain, reported to be in Washington for completing certain unspecified negotiations pending with Great Britain; negotiations presumed to relate to Anglo-American alliance.

FRIDAY, APRIL 22.

FIRST SEIZURE.

Spanish steamship Buena Ventura, laden with lumber, bound for Cuba, seized by the United States warship Nashville. (Many seizures followed, a list of them being given in the appended tables.)

Reported that Cubans familiar with the Cuban waters have been engaged for pilots of the fleet blockading the Cuban coast.

DEWEY LEAVES HONGKONG.

Commodore Dewey's fleet clears from Hongkong, accompanied by two British colliers recently purchased; cruiser Baltimore joins the fleet.

THE MONTSERRAT.

Spanish steamer Montserrat, with cargo of money, arms and ammunition, reported cleared from Canary Islands for Cuba.

American line steamer Paris, chartered by the navy, leaves Southampton, with passengers for New York; apprehension expressed that vessel will be seized by Spain.

BLOCKADE PROCLAIMED.

President proclaims blockade of north coast of Cuba, between Cardenas and Bahia Honda, and of south coast, port of Cienfuegos.

Order of Knights of Maccabees issues dispensation making order liable for benefit funds to members killed as volunteers during war. (Fraternal orders of all denominations made similar orders subsequently.)

President signs call for 125,000 volunteers.

Rock Island arsenal ordered to prepare at once field equipments for 75,000 men.

Navy Department submits bill to Congress authorizing enlistment of volunteers from naval reserves, etc.

Reported that administration intends to seize Hawaiian Islands as coaling station, etc., the Hawaiian Government approving. (Subsequently reports stated that President Dole bore with him from recent visit to Washington a bill drafted by the administration to be acted upon by Hawaiian Congress, looking to annexation to or protectorate of United States in event of Spanish-American war. Sympathy for the United States on the part of the Hawaiian public was very pronounced on all occasions, especially on the victory of Dewey at Manila. Volunteer troops for United States service were raised, coal supplies were accumulated, and various other official and semi-official acts were undertaken in the islands.)

OBSERVES THE DECLARATION OF PARIS.

Formal note as to observation of the Declaration of Paris addressed to European powers by the United States.

Reported in Great Britain that Spain has declined to observe the declaration; Spanish press declares that Spain will renounce the right of privateering.

CO-OPERATION WITH CUBAN INSURGENTS.

War Department inquires needs of the Cuban insurgents for the conduct of the war and the assistance of the United States in the repulsion of Spain. (Co-operation between the United States and the insurgents was complete from this time, the insurgent representatives placing all their resources at the command of the United States, and the

United States dispatching several preliminary expeditions of inquiry, etc., to the camps of Generals Gomez and García.)

THE QUESTION OF COAL SUPPLY.

Believed in Washington that the Spanish fleet will not hasten departure from Cape Verde because of scarcity of coal. (Scarcity of the Spanish coal supply was frequently emphasized in subsequent reports and speculations as to the movements of the fleet.)

Great Britain gives notice that coal will be considered contraband of war; Spain requests Italy not to declare coal contraband.

Reported and denied that Spanish torpedo boat Temerario has withdrawn from Buenos Ayres for attack upon the United States steamship Oregon. (The Temerario was frequently reported as having withdrawn from this port, but did not do so during the voyage of the Oregon.)

SPANISH MILITARY DICTATORSHIP.

Reported that in event of failure of the existing ministry in Spain, Marshal Campos will be called upon to form a military dictatorship.

Populace in all Spanish provinces make runs on banks to exchange currency for silver; Madrid and Barcelona bourses in panic; marked fall in Bank of Spain and other securities.

Best informed members of Spanish Cortes reported expecting unfavorable outcome of the war; same blame the administration for not being prepared.

SATURDAY, APRIL 23.

Apprehension expressed in Washington lest capture of Spanish vessel Buena Ventura—war not having been formally declared—prove contrary to international law.

GERMAN PRESS.

German press almost unanimously imputes selfish and base motives to the United States in the current situation. (This attitude was maintained consistently by a portion of the German press for a long period. It was temporarily checked by the victory of Dewey at Manila.)

Censorship of telegrams between Key West and Havana established.

House of Representatives passes a bill for the reorganization of the army. (See outline in appended tables.)

CALL FOR VOLUNTEERS.

President McKinley issues call for 125,000 volunteers to serve two years, to be furnished from each State in proportion fixed by the War Department. (See appended tables.)

Temporary army corps formed at Chickamauga; Brigadier-General Shafter assigned to command concentration at New Orleans; Coppinger at Mobile; Wade at Tampa.

PARTIES AND WAR REVENUE MEASURES.

Measure providing special taxation to provide revenue for the prosecution of the war introduced into the House by the Ways and Means Committee; measure provides for bond issues and special currency issues; Democrats oppose and protest the measure because Democratic members of Ways and Means Committee were not consulted during the preparation of the measure.

BOND ISSUE AND INCOME TAX.

Democrats of the committee propose an income tax in lieu of the bond issue.

Naval militia of several States assigned to auxiliary vessels.

Reported existence on Havana wharves of 85,000 tons of coal.

APPEALS FOR EUROPEAN INTERVENTION.

Frequent communications pass between Spain and European powers as to the existing war. (In most of the negotiations up to this date and subsequently Austria took the initiative in response to Spain's appeals, and endeavored to persuade other powers, especially Germany and Italy, to co-operate in some manner of intervention. It was reported at one time and subsequently denied that Emperor Franz Josef of Austria had made a personal contribution to the Spanish defense fund. The Pope also took the lead frequently in similar negotiations, co-operating with Austria.)

SPAIN'S CONDUCT OF WAR.

Spain publishes decree outlining conduct of war and defining contraband material; decree pledges the issuing of no letters of marque. (See outline of decree in appended tables.)

ANTI-BRITISH FEELING IN SPAIN.

Much indignation expressed in Spain against Great Britain on ground that Great Britain has secret and ulterior agreement with the United States. (Anti-British feeling increased constantly in Spain until British vessels considered it unsafe to land their crews at Spanish ports. The feeling was much intensified by the open declaration of British Secretary Chamberlain in behalf of an Anglo-American alliance. The Spanish press and officials were openly hopeful thereafter of a continental alliance, to include Spain, against the Anglo-American alliance.)

SUNDAY, APRIL 24.
FIRST SHOT.

Morro Castle at Havana fires on the United States blockading fleet without result. United States fleet makes no response.

NEUTRAL NATIONS.

Great Britain makes formal declaration of neutrality and notifies all vessels of belligerent powers to leave British ports within forty-eight hours. (The following powers subsequently proclaimed neutrality: France, Italy, Netherlands, Switzerland, Norway-Sweden, Russia, Colombia, Japan, China, Siam, Portugal, Great Britain, Mexico, Hayti, Argentine, Brazil, Belguim, Uruguay, Greece.)

FEELING AGAINST FRANCE.

Many French ship owners and some private French citizens apply for Spanish letters of marque. (This action, together with other manifestations of sympathy with Spain, especially the unfavorable attitude of the press toward the United States, created the impression that France was hostile to the United States. Much feeling was aroused in the United States against France, culminating in a concerted movement by women to boycott all French products, including articles of attire and fashion. The fact that French financiers held heavy investments in Spanish bonds w.i subseqneutly set forth as one of the motives of the temporary hostility.)

PORTUGAL AND THE CAPE VERDE FLEET.

Portuguese press manifests friendship for Spain. (Subsequently a delay in the proclamation of neutrality led to the impression that Portugal was acting in the interest of Spain; especial interest attached to the matter because of the presence of the Spanish fleet at the Portuguese Cape Verde Islands. Portugal denied acting in behalf of Spain.)

War Department decides to denominate the volunteer troops as " United States Volunteers."

MONDAY, APRIL 25.

DECLARATION OF WAR.

President McKinley transmits message to Congress recommending declaration of war to date from April 21st.

Senate and House of Representatives pass resolutions declaring war to have existed with Spain since April 21st. Bill passed in both houses without division.

Portugal notifies the Spanish fleet to leave Cape Verde Islands.

PHILIPPINE REBELS.

Reported that Philippine rebel chief Aguinaldo has arranged to sail with Dewey for the Philippines to co-operate with Dewey in the subjugation of the Spanish forces. (Aguinaldo did not sail with Dewey, but sailed subsequently under United States protection under agreement to hold action of rebels subject to direction of Dewey.)

CARRANZA'S CHALLENGE.

Lieutenant Raymond de Carranza, formerly naval attache of the Spanish legation to the United States, challenges Consul-General Lee to a duel. (This challenge was not heeded by General Lee, but a number of citizens offered to accept it in his stead. Their offers were not

Spanish Republicans endeavor to induce Castelar to lead movement for a republic.

ROCKY MOUNTAIN RIFLEMEN.

Reported that Asistant Secretary of the Navy will be appointed Lieutenant-Colonel of a regiment of mounted riflemen to be organized in the Rocky Mountains. (Roosevelt received this appointment and the regiment was organized.)

Commander John A. Wynne, retired, appointed prize commissioner to adjust seizures of vessels in Cuban blockade and elsewhere.

INCREASE OF SEAMEN IN NAVY.

Senate passes naval appropriation bill allowing enlistment of increased force during war; Senate also passes army reorganization with amendments as agreed to by conference with House committee.

QUOTAS FOR VOLUNTEERS.

War Department issues call for quota of volunteers from all States and Territories.

SHERMAN RESIGNS.

Secretary of State John Sherman resigns because of failing health. (Secretary Sherman had been practically unable to attend to his full official duties for many months past, and these matters were left largely in the hands of Asistant Secretary Day.)

TUESDAY, APRIL 26.
THE SOMERS ABANDONED.

Torpedo boat Somers abandoned in English port because of failure to complete repairs prior to British declaration of neutrality.

Madrid El Liberal, organ of ministry, intimates that Spanish policy will be to act in defense of territory, not withdrawing from same to engage the United States until first attacked.

RUNNING THE BLOCKADE.

Reported that Spanish steamer Montserrat has run the Cuban blockade, landed cargo and escaped. (Spain subsequently claimed that the Montserrat ran the blockade three times; it was reported that this fact would be used by Spain to protest to the European powers that the blockade was not effective. The commander of the Montserrat was given a public ovation upon his return to Madrid after the alleged third running of the blockade.)

AFTER THE FIRST CONFLICT.

Reported that Austria and Germany have agreed to intervene after first serious encounter of the war. (Similar reports were frequent even after the battle of Manila. The new Cabinet in Spain late in May declared that such intervention was entirely likely.)

Spanish forces abandon Moron Jucaco trocha in Cuba to the insurgents. (The Spaniards subsequently practically abandoned all interior strongholds and concentrated forces on the coast.)

UNITED STATES' CONDUCT OF THE WAR.

President McKinley issues proclamation defining United States conduct of the war, including policy as to privateering.

A NEW SECRETARY OF STATE.

William R. Day of Ohio appointed Secretary of State; John Bassett Moore of Columbia University appointed Assistant Secretary of State. (The affairs of the State Department, owing to the illness of Secretary Sherman, had been largely in Mr. Day's hands as assistant secretary for many months.)

AN INCOME TAX.

Measure to provide revenue for the conduct of the war submitted from the House Committee on Ways and Means; Bailey presents Democratic substitute for bond issue provision of the measure, substitute providing an income tax and directing coinage of the seignorage in the Treasury.

Explosion destroys portion of California Powder Works, engaged in manufacture of Government material. (Suspicion of Spanish agency attached to this explosion, but no conclusive evidence to that effect was obtained.)

WEDNESDAY, APRIL 27.

THE MATANZAS ENGAGEMENT AND SPANISH MARKSMANSHIP.

Spanish batteries at Matanzas fire upon United States blockading fleet; United States vessels New York, Puritan and Cincinnati return the fire; Spanish batteries silenced within twenty minutes; Spanish guns fail to hit the United States vessels. (This failure of Spanish marksmanship was noted in numerous subsequent engagements, including the battle of Manila; the crews of the defeated fleet at Manila stated that they had had no target practice for two years.)

"GUAGE BUOYS."

(The Spanish errancy in this regard finally led to the placing of "gauge buoys" indicating the shooting range from the fortifications; the Spanish guns reserved their fire until the United States vessels reached the buoys. Severe damage was done to the United States torpedo boat Winslow by this strategy.)

Hongkong (Dewey's) fleet sails from Mirs bay, China, for Manila; Consul-General Williams states that Philippine rebels surround Manila.

Reported that Spanish fleet sailed from Cape Verde on April 26th.

FUTURE INTERNATIONAL POLICY OF THE UNITED STATES.

German Socialist Democratic Leader Liebkneckt declares that the United States has overstepped its traditional policy of neutrality and will not end its interference in international affairs with the dispute with Spain. (Apprehension of the possible future international policy of the United States became universal in European countries from this time and added much to the agitation for a continental alliance. The victory of Dewey at Manila and the probable necessity of the retention of the islands seemed to confirm the European apprehension.)

PRIZE COURT.

Prize court of inquiry convenes at Jacksonville, Fla., with G. R. Bowen Patterson as president.

HELEN GOULD'S GIFT.

Helen Gould, daughter of the late noted financier, Jay Gould, tenders $100,000 to the Government for use in defaying the expenses of the war.

SPANISH SEIZURE.

American bark Saranac captured off the Philippines by the Spanish naval vessels. (This was the only seizure of importance reported by the Spanish navy.)

RESPONSE OF THE MILITIA.

Militia of all States respond to call for volunteers. (This response was prompt, most States reporting ready to respond to summons for service within forty-eight hours. In some instances companies and regiments protested against enlistment except upon guarantee of being able to retain their own officers; in several instances where this was not guaranteed the regiments refused to enlist, notably in the case of the "famous Seventh" Regiment of New York. In one State the refusal of a company to enlist was followed by their summary disbandment by the Governor, women and girls seizing the men's uniforms and desiring to enlist in their places.)

Debate on the war revenue measure begun in the House of Representatives; absence of partisan feeling noted; Democrats and Populists consistently opposed and voted against the bond issue.

President McKinley signs the army reorganization bill.

BANKERS AND THE BOND ISSUE.

Secretary of the Treasury Gage consults with New York bankers with reference to proposed bond issue; bankers signify desire to have bonds bear $3\frac{1}{2}$ per cent interest; Gage insists that only 3 per cent will be allowed.

Spanish press declares that tardiness of United States in beginning actual hostilities indicates weakness.

THURSDAY, APRIL 28.

GERMANY AND THE PHILIPPINES.

State Department unofficially advised that Germany will interfere with bombardment of Manila. (This rumor was persistently repeated against German denials. German interest in the Philippines and probable action antagonistic to United States retention of the islands was continuously emphasized in press reports.)

TROOPS ORDERED TO TAMPA.

Troops ordered from Chickamauga, New Orleans and Mobile to Tampa; presumably to prepare for immediate invasion of Cuba. (Concentration of troops and other preparations for Cuban invasion continued at Tampa until the arrival of the Spanish fleet at Martinique, when they were temporarily suspended.)

Eight large steamers chartered to convey troops to Cuba. (A total number of thirty transport ships were ultimately engaged for this purpose.)

Spanish fleet at Philippines puts into Subig bay north of Manila. (The fleet was ordered back to Manila immediately prior to the arrival of Dewey's fleet.)

Naval bureau chiefs decide to invite bids for three battleships similar to the Illinois.

FOREIGN AMERICAN VOLUNTEERS.

Secretary Alger refuses to modify allotment of volunteer call among States in response to requests of Congressmen and others.

Colony of Russian Jewish farmers in New Jersey volunteers for war service. (Volunteers were offered from all classes of foreign Americans, including a completely equipped regiment of experienced Canadian Americans.)

COMPARATIVE MERITS OF NAVIES.

British naval critic W. Laird Clowes declares Spanish navy superior to the United States navy in torpedo flotilla, but weaker in larger craft; considers natural and acquired fighting qualities of Americans superior; thinks Spain cannot afford to risk her ships in American harbors. (Clowes' opinion was repeated in effect by other British naval experts, including Sir Philip Columb.)

Porto Rico reported to have received sufficient supplies to withstand a siege of two months.

Rush order issued by War Department for six additional disappearing gun carriages.

PROTEST AGAINST TONNAGE TAX.

Protest offered in British Parliament against provision for tonnage tax on merchant marine in war revenue bill pending in the United States Congress. (This protest was promptly recognized and the provision was omitted from the bill by the Senate.)

Rush order for 200 13-inch projectiles of weight of 1100 pounds each issued by Navy Department. (This order was filled by May 22d, when 100 of the projectiles were forwarded to the fleet of Admiral Sampson in Cuban waters.)

Officially announced in Spain that the fleet has withdrawn from Cape Verde.

BRITISH SENTIMENT NOT DIVIDED.

Denied that British sentiment is divided against the United States. (The reports were circulated freely that British sentiment was reacting in favor of Spain. This report was actively combated by Alfred Harmsworth of the London press, who showed by percentage count a large preponderance of opinion in favor of the United States, even among Tories. Hostility to the United States seemed to have entirely vanished by the time of the Birmingham speech by Secretary Chamberlain.)

SPANISH REPORTS OF AMERICAN REVERSES.

Spanish official dispatches declare defeat and repulse of United States fleet at Matanzas. (The repulse of the United States fleet was reported from Spain in connection with every engagement except the battle of Manila. False reports were persistently given out by Captain-General Blanco representing many disasters to United States vessels.)

Price of wheat reported higher in England than within twenty years past.

FRIDAY, APRIL 29.

Anxiety felt in Navy Department lest Spanish fleet from Cape Verde attempt to overhaul the battleship Oregon en route north on South American coast.

SPANISH SPIES AND THE SECRET SERVICE.

United States Secret Service in all parts of the country

instructed to watch for Spanish spies. (Two suspects had been arrested up to date. Numerous arrests on suspicion ensued from this date. Former Spanish Minister Bernabe, who had withdrawn to Canada, appeared to be directing an elaborate system of spies from Canadian territory. Bernabe was finally requested to withdraw from Canada.)

A RECONNOISANCE.

Admiral Sampson advises Navy Department of attack on Matanzas; brevity of advices indicates that attack was merely a reconnoisance.

Reported that Spanish General Parrado in Havana has perfected plan for re-conquest of Florida.

FIRING OFF NEW ENGLAND COAST.

Heavy gun-firing heard off Quoddy Heads, Mass. (Reports of this character from the New England coast were frequent during subsequent days, usually leading to belief that portion of Spanish fleet was off the coast in pursuance of the announced plan of Spain to attack American coast cities instead of defending Cuba.)

Reports from Porto Rico indicate famine and violent disorder, with arbitrary efforts of Spanish authorities to suppress the disaffection.

LOYALTY OF SOUTHERN STATES.

Noted in New Orleans that ex-Confederates are most willing volunteers in response to President's call. (The co-operation of the South in the movement against Spain was assured in various speeches in Congress and emphasized by Consul-General Lee in his public utterances at the ovations tendered him on his return from Cuba. At no time was any disaffection expressed, except by General Wade Hampton some time prior to the war and when war was not expected, Hampton stating that the South was too busy with reconstruction to be interested in martial affairs.)

WAR REVENUE BILL PASSED.

House passes war revenue bill by vote of 181 to 131; Democratic motion to strike out provision for bond issue defeated by vote of 134 to 173.

WAR DEFICIENCY.

Secretary of War transmits estimate of deficiency of $34,019,997 for balance of fiscal year, due to war expenditures.

PRICES ADVANCE.

Lack of excitement or nervousness and interruption in trade circles owing to war noted by trade journals. Continued marking up of prices of all classes of commodities noted by trade journals.

NO NAVAL NEWS.

Secretary of War issues sweeping instructions to department against giving out information of naval movements.

SATURDAY, APRIL 30.

Reported that European powers expect occupation of Philippines as one of first acts of the United States and that the powers do not contemplate interference.

Navy Department expects false reports of Dewey's actions at Manila because of control of cables by the Spanish authorities. (The first advices of Dewey's victory on the subsequent day were received through Spanish sources, the reports showing no endeavor to belittle the victory.)

RUSSIA AND THE PHILIPPINES.

Reported that Russia is not likely to allow the United States to retain the Philippines. (This report was circulated subsequently with the same persistency as was the report of German intentions. Russia made no official announcements in the matter.)

Battleship Oregon arrives safely at Rio Janeiro, having made average record of $11\frac{3}{4}$ knots from Callao.

German press publishes reports of many disasters to United States warships. (The German press continued reports of this character; it was also usually twelve hours tardy in reports of authentic news; it maintained unfavorable opinion of the United States navy, varying the opinion for a short while subsequent to battle at Manila.)

LATINS VS. ANGLO-SAXONS.

Paris, Rome and Portuguese press point out that Spain

ish-American war is a conflict between Latins and Anglo-Saxons; German papers show disposition on this account to favor the Anglo-American alliance.

Papal nuncios in Germany reported as stating that the Pope acted in Spanish-American matter on misinformation; he should have asked that Cuba be ceded to the Pope, the Pope to give the islands to the Cubans.

A NEW DREIBUND.

German Socialist Liebknecht declares that a new Dreibund, including Great Britain, United States and Japan is springing into existence. (This triple alliance was frequently mentioned in press and diplomatic circles subsequently.)

GERMAN COMMERCE.

Wheat advances in Germany to 221 marks.

Many American orders with German exporters countermanded. (This movement subsequently became so extensive that German exporters made great efforts to counteract the anti-American sentiment throughout Germany; they succeeded in altering the hostile attitude of numerous important newspapers.)

Quartermaster and commissary officers for the volunteers assigned.

ENGAGEMENT AT CABANAS—MASKED BATTERIES.

Spanish batteries at Cabanas fire at the United States blockading fleet; fleet returns fire, silencing Spanish batteries after first shot. (Numerous small engagements of this character ensued during the blockade, the Spanish forces frequently firing from masked batteries. The United States vessels were surprised several times by the existence of the masked batteries.)

SUNDAY, MAY 1.
THE BATTLE OF MANILA.

United States fleet, under Commodore Dewey, completely defeats and destroys Spanish fleet in Manila harbor, under Admiral Montijo, after sharp and furious battle, lasting two hours. (Subsequent advices from Dewey state the

United States vessels were almost uninjured and that only eight men were wounded, none being killed or fatally wounded. Subsequent Spanish estimates placed the Spanish loss at 300 killed and between 600 and 700 wounded. The skillful maneuvering of the United States vessels and the bad markmanship of the Spanish guns, both on the vessels and in the forts, account for the immunity of the United States ships and men.)

DEWEY'S GREAT VICTORY.

During the engagement Dewey destroyed the Spanish naval station Cavite and the fortifications at the entrance to the bay of Manila; then occupied Cavite and established complete blockade of the harbor, reporting himself in position to capture the city of Manila at any time.

POPULAR RESENTMENT IN SPAIN.

Early dispatches in Madrid claim that the battle of Manila was a Spanish victory, but upon subsequent reversal of the report excited crowds gathered in the streets threatening riot. (Riots subsequently followed throughout Spain. The protest of the public against the defeat of Admiral Montijo and the annihilation of his fleet was aggravated by outbreak of bread riots. Martial law and military discipline were required to suppress the disorders, together with official repeal of the import tax upon grains and many extensive philanthropic plans for the relief of the sufferers from the high prices of grain and bread. For some time immediate revolution, with overthrow of the dynasty, seemed imminent. The movement culminated, apparntly, in the resignation of the existing ministry and the appointment of a Cabinet pledged to most vigorous foreign and colonial measures.)

EFFECTS OF THE VICTORY.

Opinion reported prevailing in Washington official circles that decisive victory of Dewey presages early termination of the war; also increase of United States prestige abroad, and establishment of European sympathy with the United States.

HURRYING THE CUBAN INVASION.

Reported that Dewey's victory will hasten the bombard

ment of Havana and the invasion of Cuba. (The invasion of Cuba was subsequently postponed to permit of greater concentration of troops in the South for the purpose, and again postponed owing to the uncertainty as to the location of the Spanish fleet from Cape Verde, and still again owing to the definite news of the arrival of the Cape Verde fleet in West Indian waters. United States naval and military preparations and movements subsequent to this date were on a comprehensive scale. They are indicated in the tables of army and navy organization and mobilization appended hereto.)

MONDAY, MAY 2.

SPANISH BRAVERY.

Additional advices indicate that the Spanish crews at Manila fought with great bravery. (Commodore Dewey, and other officers and men of the United States fleet expressed their congratulations to Admiral Montijo and his men for their gallant resistance.)

PRAISE FOR DEWEY.

Universal admiration expressed in England for the daring and strategy of Dewey. (This admiration took the form of most elaborate enconiums, ranking Dewey among the world's great naval commanders, "a worthy successor of Perry and Farragut." The enconiums were also extended by German officials, including Emperor William who remarked after perusing accounts of the battle that there "evidently is something in these Yankees besides smartness and commercialism."

AMERICAN CREWS.

Conviction expressed in Washington that the battle of Manila disproves European contention that heterogeneity of crews of United States navy would operate to prevent discipline and effective fighting power.

Four German warships reported already en route or dispatched to the Philippines. (European powers were subsequently reported as looking with disfavor upon this movement.)

TRANSPORTATION.

War Department intimates to all railroads that it will not pay more than one cent per mile passenger fare for the transportation of troops. (This was the rate paid during the Civil War.)

IMMUNES TO YELLOW FEVER.

Senate passes bills for enlistment of brigade of volunteer engineers and of 10,000 special volunteers who are immune to yellow fever. (These bills passed both houses and became laws.)

THE LAST OF THE MAINE.

Reported that Spanish authorities have blown up the hull of the battleship Maine, remaining in Havana harbor.

TUESDAY, MAY 3.

CONTENTIONS IN THE SPANISH CORTES.

Extraordinary excitement attends reopening of the Spanish Cortes; Republican leader, Professor Salmoren, passionately demands explanation of the disaster at Manila; Republicans and Carlists violently demonstrative. (Republicans and Carlists led the criticism of the Government until the formation of the new ministry late in the month. Both parties made speeches directed toward the overthrow of the existing dynasty. Weyler, the former Captain-General of Cuba, was associated in one manner or another with the campaign of these parties, being announced at one time as a member of the provisional ministry formed by Don Carlos in the event of his seizure of the throne.)

EXPEDITION TO THE PHILIPPINES.

Mobilization of 10,000 volunteers at San Francasco ordered at once; the cruiser Charleston, at Mare Island Navy Yard, ordered to hasten preparations for departure to the Philippines to the relief of Dewey (San Francisco from this time became the center of a general movement for the re-enforcement of Dewey.)

Tests by cable company indicate that the cable to Manila was cut prior to the Manila battle at a point about fifty fifty miles from shore. (Subsequent advices stated that the cable was cut by Commodore Dewey. Dewey's official advices of the Manila battle were forwarded to Hongkong by the dispatch boat McCulloch and cabled from that point to Washington.)

DISPOSITION OF THE PHILIPPINES.

European diplomats at Washington discuss the probable disposition of the Philippines after the present occupation by the United States.

REFUGE FOR THE QUEEN REGENT.

Reported that Spanish Queen Regent and her family in Austria (Emperor Franz Josef being the brother) are corresponding as to advisability of Queen Regent abdicating the regency to save the throne for her son, the present King. (Rumors to this effect, together with rumors that quarters had been prepared for the reception of the Spanish royal family in event of forced flight from Spain in Austria, were persistently circulated and as persistently denied throughout April and May.)

WEDNESDAY, MAY 4.
SAMPSON'S FLEET SETS SAIL.

United States fleet, under Admiral Sampson, sails from Key West, presumably to meet Spanish fleet from Cape Verde or to capture the Spanish coal supplies at San Juan de Porto Rico before the arrival of the Cape Verde fleet. (Sampson subsequently bombarded or engaged the forts at San Juan, but did not capture the Spanish coal supplies.)

ARMY APPOINTMENTS.

President nominates eleven Major-Generals of the army, including seven Brigadier-Generals and four civilians; civilians include former Consul-General Fitzhugh Lee. (These were the first of a long list of nominations in army and navy made by the President in placing the army upon a war footing. A complete list of the appointments is appended.)

FOREIGN NAVAL AND MILITARY OBSERVATIONS.

Numerous foreign military and naval representatives are

rive in Washington to accompany United States troops and vessels in war movements, for the purpose of observation.

EXTRAORDINARY ILLUSTRATION OF SEA POWER.

British Vice-Admiral, Sir Philip Howard Columb, declares the battle of Manila the most extraordinary illustration of sea power ever made, and considers that the United States navy, after the success at Manila, is not likely to be willing to accept subordinate rank among the navies of the world.

THURSDAY, MAY 5.

EXPANSION OF NATIONAL TERRITORY.

Senator Gorman quoted as stating that Hawaii and the Philippine Islands are necessary to the naval power and commerce of the United States in the Orient; Senator Lodge quoted as urging similar views. (The absorption of the Hawaiian and Philippine Islands rapidly became a subject of general discussion after this time, eventually indicating the possible rise of a general political issue on the expansion of United States terirtory.

NATIONS PERMIT ANNEXATION OF HAWAII.

Japanese Minister at Washington states, after conference at the State Department, that Japan will accept Hawaiian annexation to the United States in a friendly spirit. (Prior announcement that Great Britain had no intention whatever to seek interest in the islands, together with this declaration by Japan, freed the question of the annexation of the islands by the United States from international complications. A report was published, entirely without confirmation, that in the settlement of the peace with Spain, Germany would demand one of the Hawaiian Islands, a coaling station in the Philippines and the cession of Samoa in entirety as condition of acceding to the retention of the Philippines by the United States. Diplomatic circles paid no apparent attention to the report.)

FRIDAY, MAY 6.

GREAT BRITAIN AND THE PHILIPPINES.

Well-informed circles in London reported as regarding arrangements determined between the United States and Great Britain as to the disposition of the Philippines. (The conviction that such was the case was subsequently reported to be general on the continent of Europe. In some circles it was believed that the United States had agreed to cede the Philippines to Great Britain in exchange for the British West Indies. A prominent member of the British Parliament was quoted as declaring the possible exchange too good to be true.)

NEW SENSE OF NATIONAL STRENGTH.

Bradstreet's commercial paper reports that the new sense of national strength following the battle of Manila has checked the business depression which had been consequent upon the movements of the war with Spain up to this date. (By the end of the third week in May general trade was reported to have attained a very large volume, the indications of strong industrial outlook at that time exerting a marked influence on the stock exchange.)

SATURDAY, MAY 7.

Official advices received from Commodore Dewey as to the battle of Manila. (See full cablegram in appendix.)

CENTRALISM AND IMPERIALISM.

German Kreuz Zeitung expresses belief that current Spanish-American war will strengthen centralism and imperialism in the United States.

CAUSES OF DEWEY'S VICTORY.

Naval authorities at Washington attribute Dewey's victory to "superior gunnery, target practice, coolness, preparedness."

May wheat advances in Chicago Board of Trade to $1.70 per bushel; best flour advances to $7.40 per barrel; Joseph Leiter and his foreign customers continue to hold the supply.

SUNDAY, MAY 9.

Battleship Oregon reported to have arrived at Bahia in Brazil. (Subsequent advices indicated that the Oregon arrived at Bahia prior to this date and departed May 8th, the false report of this date being intended to deceive the Spanish authorities to prevent capture of the vessel by the Spanish fleet.)

PRELIMINARY CUBAN EXPEDITION.

Lieutenant Andrew S. Rowan returns from an expedition to Cuba for conference with the insurgent General, Calixto Garcia, with reference to co-operation of the insurgents with the United States in expelling the Spanish forces. (Rowan's expedition was one of several expeditions forwarded for similar purposes, news of which was subsequently suppressed by the Government censorship of telegrams. One expedition, under Captain J. H. Dorst, failed to effect a landing, alleging that Cuban insurgents did not keep agreement to meet the landing party; party was repulsed by Spanish cavalry.)

ALLEN SUCCEEDS ROOSEVELT.

Charles H. Allen of Massachusetts appointed first Assistant Secretary of State to succeed Theodore Roosevelt, resigned. (The statement was made, without confirmation, that Roosevelt's resignation was due partially to impatience with the conservative policy of the Navy Department.)

DEWEY THANKED AND PROMOTED.

President McKinley transmits message to Congress recommending extension of gratitude to Commodore Dewey and giving notice that Dewey has been appointed acting Rear-Admiral in recognition of his services at the battle of Manila.

Senate and House of Representatives unanimously extend gratitude to Dewey, and pass resolutions increasing the number of Rear-Admirals from six to seven to allow for the promotion of Dewey, and the striking of bronze medals for the officers and crew of his fleet.

TUESDAY, MAY 10.

State Department announces receipt of official advices that the Spanish fleet from Cape Verde has returned to Cadiz. (The New York Journal claimed to have obtained this information and to have furnished it to the authorities. The United States naval attache at London reported doubt of the accuracy of the information and his doubt was confirmed a few days later by the appearance of the fleet at the island of Martinique, in the French West Indies. Press reports indicated that the movements of the fleet of Admiral Sampson were altered in accordance with the report of the return of the Spanish fleet to Cadiz, but the reports were not confirmed officially. The bombardment of San Juan de Porto Rico by Admiral Sampson's fleet followed two days later, reports subsequently alleging that Admiral Sampson approached the Porto Rico harbor expecting to find the Spanish fleet stationed there.)

HIGH WHEAT.

May wheat advances to $1.75 in Chicago, $1.90 at New York, $1.80 at Detroit and $1.60 at Minneapolis.

CATHOLIC PRAYERS FOR AMERICAN SUCCESS.

Archbishops of the Catholic Church in the United States issue circular letters directing prayers in all churches for the success of the United States in the present war. (The activity of Pope Leo in negotiations with the Spanish Queen Regent and Austrian Emperor looking to the peacable adjustment of the Spanish-American controversy created the impression in some circles that Catholic sympathy as a whole lay with Spain. American Catholics resented this imputation. Some influential Catholics were reported to have urged the Pope to discontinue his efforts at mediation because of the misinterpretation of his action likely to be made by persons in the United States hostile to the Catholic Church.)

PAYING OUT GOLD.

United States Treasury begins paying out gold in lieu of currency; cash balance in the Treasury, $213,313,585; gold reserve, $180,428,261. (Up to this date the extraordinary expenses of the war had not been allowed to invade the Government gold reserve, which had been constantly increasing for nearly a year past.)

WEDNESDAY, MAY 11.
SPANISH EXPEDITION TO THE PHILIPPINES.

Officially announced that a naval and military expedition is being organized in Spain to expel Admiral Dewey from the Philippines. (Numerous reports of the definite starting of this expedition were circulated during the next two weeks in the same manner in which conflicting reports of the departure of the Cape Verde fleet from Cape Verde were circulated. Statements were also made that the fleet and troops were destined to effect juncture with Cervera in the West Indies. The definite time of the starting of the expedition or its destination were not ascertained prior to their being reported at other than Spanish ports.)

MERRITT TO BE GOVERNOR OF THE PHILIPPINES.

Major-General Merritt designated to the command of the expedition to the Philippines and to the military Governorship of the islands, pending their final disposition.

Infantry from Wyoming, Colorado, Kansas, Montana, Nebraska, North Dakota and Idaho, and light artillery and cavalry from Utah ordered to San Francisco. (This was the beginning of a large movement of troops to San Francisco for the purpose of dispatch to the Philippines. General Merritt requested and was allowed additional forces of regulars and of experienced volunteers, and the expedition ultimately assumed a large scope.)

REBELS SEEK AMERICAN CITIZENSHIP.

Philippine rebel refugees in Hongkong prepare a congratulatory address to Admiral Dewey; the address prays for an independent native government under the protection of the United States; Rebel Chief Aguinaldo issues a proclamation directing obedience to Admiral Dewey; frequent applications are made by rebels in Hongkong for admission to United States citizenship.

Major-General Brooke instructed to prepare for concentration at Chickamauga of 40,000 to 50,000 volunteers.

SENATE COMMITTEE AGAINST BOND ISSUE. CORPORATION TAX.

Senate Finance Committee, by deciding vote of Senator Jones of Nevada, strikes out the bond provision from the war revenue bill and substitutes provision for $\frac{1}{4}$ of 1 per cent tax on incomes of corporations, provision for coinage of the seignorage in the Treasury, and for issuance of $150,000,000 in greenbacks. (Democrats, Populists and many of the Silver Republicans sustained these substitutions during the debate that followed in the Senate; Republicans generally were against the change from the original form of the House bill.)

President McKinley nominates and the Senate immediately confirms acting Rear-Admiral Dewey to be Rear-Admiral.

STOCKS MOVE UPWARD.

Upward movement sets in on the New York stock exchange. (This was subsequently held in check by the absolute censorship upon all war news by the War and Navy departments.)

THURSDAY, MAY 12.

Sampson's fleet, while reconnoitering at San Juan de Porto Rico for the presence of the Spanish fleet, is fired upon and returns the fire; a general bombardment ensues until Spanish guns are partially silenced. Sampson thereupon withdraws. (Subsequent reports indicated that comparatively slight damage was done to the forts, a few guns being dislodged and a few Spaniards being wounded and killed.)

ENGAGEMENT AT SAN JUAN DE PORTO RICO.

Gunboat Winslow badly damaged by shell from Spanish batteries at Cardenas; Ensign Worth Bagley killed, together with four of the crew; Lieutenant John B. Bernadou and two men wounded; Winslow had been dispatched to ascertain the nature of certain vessels, presumably gunboats, in the Cardenas harbor. " Gauge buoys" were used by the Spanish forts in directing their guns at the Winslow.

EUROPEAN COMBINATION AGAINST GREAT BRITAIN AND THE UNITED STATES.

St. James Gazette of London declares that movements of European nations portend combination against the United States and Great Britain, Europe believing that the United States is only trying its strength on Spain and that Great Britain is associated with the United States in aggression against Continental Europe; the Gazette warns Great Britain to prepare for a struggle involving the most important events since the period of Napoleon.

SPEED OF SPAIN'S FLEET.

Flying squadron under Commodore Schley departs from Hampton Roads to join Cuban blockading fleet or to reenforce Sampson's fleet.

Technical comparisons indicate superiority of Sampson's fleet over the Spanish fleet, but superiority of Spanish fleet in speed. (The subsequent maneuvers of Sampson's and Schley's fleet appeared to be calculated to overcome strategically the superior speed of the Spanish fleet.)

FRIDAY, MAY 13

CHAMBERLAIN'S SPEECH AT BIRMINGHAM.

British Secretary of State for Colonies, Joseph Chamberlain, delivers speech at Birmingham stating that Great Britain may soon be confronted by a combination of powers, urging maintenance of bonds of permanent unity with the "kinsmen beyond the sea," declaring that Russia is ineligible to alliance because of perfidy, and holding that Great Britain must depend for retention of position in the Orient upon alliance with some nation whose interests are mutual . (This speech was discussed in all diplomatic circles and held to be a critical utterance in the existing international situation. Its open bid for an Anglo-American alliance intensified the anti-British sentiment in Spain and stimulated the efforts and hopes of that country for either a continental alliance of a Franco-Spanish alliance. The bid for the Anglo-American alliance, together with the intimidation of an impending combination against Great Britain, were the most widely discussed features of the speech.)

TRIPLE REPUBLIC.

Editor Henri Rochefort of the Paris Intransigeant suggests the conversion of Spain and Italy into republics and the formation of a tripartite republic of France, Spain and Italy.

NO COAL FOR SPANISH VESSELS.

Spanish fleet reported off island of Curacoa. (The fleet secured coal and provisions at this port and was next reported at Santiago de Cuba. The United States protested against the coaling and provisioning at a neutral port, and Curacoa was thereafter closed to the fleet. The entire West Indies, excepting only the Spanish ports, were closed to Cervera for coal and supplies.)

SATURDAY, MAY 14.

RE-SHAPING OF NATIONAL POLITICS.

Press reports from London assert that upon the response of the United States to the invitation of Great Britain for an alliance depends the shaping of the future politics of all European nations; that European nations anticipate the downfall of Spain and object to the United States securing any of the spoils outside of the West Indies; that European attitude has now become hostile to the entire Anglo-Saxon race.

CRITICAL POSITION OF THE UNITED STATES.

Press reports also state that Great Britain is ready to negotiate either complete or partial offensive and defensive alliance with the United States; that Great Britain especially urges the United States to promptly equip as a first-class naval power. (A few days later Andrew Carnegie in an interview on the proposed Anglo-American alliance called to public attention a phrase previously used by former Secretary of State Olney as being now substantiable, namely, the phrase "race patriotism.")

SUNDAY, MAY 15.

SPANISH CABINET RESIGNS.

Members of the Spanish Cabinet resign.

Spanish torpedo boat Terror and hospital ship Alicante

detained at Martinique (Fort de France) for repairs and not allowed to coal.

MONDAY, MAY 16,

WAR EXPENSES.

War Department estimates war expenditures to July 1, 1899, at $150,925,527; Navy Department estimates expenditures at $75,556,250.

COMPLAINT AGAINST STRATEGIC BOARD.

Reported that President McKinley will take initiative in war movements from the Strategic Board and direct movements personally. (Much complaint against the alleged tardiness of the Strategic Board by naval officers and by Congressmen was reported both prior to and subsequent to this time. Complaint was made in many sources at the delay of the bombardment of Havana until the arrival of the Spanish fleet, when the hazardousness of the undertaking was much increased.)

BERNABE'S SYSTEM OF SPIES.

Former Spanish Minister Bernabe reported to be carrying on an elaborate system of spies in the United States through headquarters at Montreal. (The Governor-General of Canada, presumably upon representation of the United States, subsequently requested Bernabe to withdraw from Canada; Bernabe accordingly withdrew. Former Charge d'Affaires De Bosc remained in charge of the headquarters.)

Assignment of Major-Generals to the respective army corps and departments.

TUESDAY, MAY 17.

FLEETS REFORMED.

Reported that Sampson's and Schley's fleets are to be reconstituted, the heavier vessels, battleships, monitors, etc., to be placed in squadron under Sampson, the cruisers, etc., to be placed under Schley.

Transmission of cable and telegraphic reports of movements of the United States fleets absolutely forbidden.

HAWAII DELAYED.

Foreign committee of the House of Representatives favorably reports Newland's resolution for the annexation of the Hawaiian Islands. (The consideration of this measure was held over by Speaker Reed pending the completion in the Senate and final disposal in the House of the war revenue measure.)

WEDNESDAY, MAY 18.
SAFETY OF THE OREGON.

Navy Department announces that the battleship Oregon is safe, but refuses to state the vessel's present location.

CUTTING CUBAN CABLES.

Auxiliary cruiser St. Louis and tug Wampatuck cut the cables at Santiago de Cuba and Guantanamo under fire of forts; shots from vessels practically silence the forts.

USING TH EENEMY'S FLAG.

General Blanco reports to Madrid that the United States vessels tried to enter Santiago harbor under Spanish flag. (This action was strongly protested in the Spanish Cortes during the following week and formally laid before the powers for consideration as a violation of the laws of war.)

THURSDAY, MAY 19.
SPAIN'S FLEET AT SANTIAGO.

Spanish fleet reported arrived at Santiago de Cuba, two United States vessels retreating upon the arrival of the Spanish vessels.

Reported that Spain has secured coaling station on the Island of St. Pierre and Miquelon in mouth of St. Lawrence river.

New Cabinet appointed in Spain.

FRIDAY, MARCH 20.
CERVERA'S SKILL.

Secretary Long quoted as expecting naval battle in West Indies within forty-eight hours. Naval officers recognize skill of Spanish Admiral, Cervera, as a sailor.

Reported that United States fleets have proceeded on

either side of Cuba to enclose Spanish fleet in Santiago.

NEW SPANISH CABINET FOR VIGOROUS WAR.

New Spanish Cabinet announces intention to prosecute the war with vigor.

Reported that Spanish Ambassador to France is negotiating for an alliance of some sort, either with France or with the Franco-Russian alliance, or with the Continental powers.

SATURDAY, MAY 21.

FRENCH SYMPATHY SHIFTS.

Shifting of French sentiment toward the United States noted in the French press; also praise of United States naval movements; French shopkeepers much perturbed by the boycott of French products by American women.

NO UNIVERSAL CONFLICT.

Paris Temps declares that the idea of universal conflict growing out of the Spanish-American war is ridiculous.

Excess reserve in New York associated banks indicates re-accumulation of money at that center; small expanse in loans indicates beginning of some new business activity.

SUNDAY, MAY 22.

SPAIN ANTICIPATED DEFEAT.

Spanish Minister of the Interior declares that Spain undertook the war with full knowledge of the superiority of the United States, but did so in defense of national honor.

RUSSIAN FRIENDSHIP.

Reported that Russia has determined not to associate herself with any anti-American pressure.

BRITISH ALLIANCE WITH JAPAN.

Vienna reports state that Great Britain has made advances to Japan with reference to all Eastern matters and possible eventualities of the Spanish-American war, thus effecting new balance of power in the Orient.

MONDAY, MAY 23.
APPEAL TO AMERICAN MAGNANIMITY.

Anonymous veteran diplomat at Madrid quoted as predicting that European powers will intervene in the Spanish-American war so soon as it has reached a point that will warrant the powers in appealing to the magnanimity of the United States.

FRANCO-SPANISH ALLIANCE.

Several leading dealers in the London Stock Exchange claim to have information that a Franco-Spanish alliance will shortly be effected.

Gray-brown linen uniform substituted for the regulation United States army blue, for the invasion of Cuba.

INSURGENTS APPROACH THE CUBAN COAST.

Cuban insurgents reported to be fighting their way to the coast to meet invading United States troops.

MANEUVERS OF THE VOLUNTEERS.

Review of volunteers of First Division of First Corps at Chickamauga shows remarkable rapidity and precision of action; officers much gratified.

FULL CONTROL OF PHILIPPINES.

Treasury Department prepares regulations for military collection of customs in the Philippines. Reported that complete control of the islands is intended, and that General Merritt will proclaim martial law.

First Regiment of California Volunteers embarks for the Philippines.

TUESDAY, MAY 24.

CEVERA BLOCKADED.

Spanish fleet believed to be enclosed in Santiago harbor by fleets of Sampson and Schley.

Dewey reports great scarcity of provisions and disorder among Spanish volunteers in Manila; rebels preparing to assist the United States.

Dewey declines to allow a German merchant ship to land supplies at Manila; foreign residents remove to Cavite.

PEACE.

Reported that Spain will accept proposition of any neutral power looking to negotiations for honorable peace.

NO WASTE OF LIFE.

General Miles, commanding the United States army, declares that no precipitate movements likely to involve waste of life will be made.

WEDNESDAY, MAY 25.
OFF FOR MANILA.

Expedition embarks from San Francisco for the Philippines; contains First California and First Oregon Volunteers and six companies of Fourteenth regular infantry, with two detachments of volunteer heavy artillery.

MORE VOLUNTEERS.

President McKinley issues call for 75,000 additional volunteers to be furnished by the several States in proportion to population, but without special application to the militia. (The partial aim of this call was to allow the President to avail himself of the numerous private and special regiments raised and equipped in various portions of the United States.)

THURSDAY, MAY 26.
ARMY OF INVASION.

Formation of all troops in Florida into corps, divisions and brigades completed; army for invasion of Cuba now organized.

COALING IN HAWAII.

Reported that Germany and France will protest against the Hawaiian Government allowing the coaling of the vessels on the United States expedition to the Philippines as a violation of neutrality.

TAXATION AWAITS NAVAL RESULTS.

Senators Teller and Daniel withhold consent from proposition to set date for voting on the war revenue measure, on ground that the issue in the West Indies should be awaited before the additional taxation is levied.

FRIDAY, MAY 27.
EFFECT OF MANILA BLOCKADE.

Commodore Schley's fleet reported to have blockaded

port of Cienfuegos, under mistaken impression that the Spanish fleet was within.

Scarcity of food increases in Manila, owing to the blockade maintained by Dewey.

Former Captain-General of the Philippines, Marshal Rivera, declares that Spain refused to re-enforce the islands because of hope that the mediation of the Pope would avert rupture with the United States.

SATURDAY, MAY 28.
BLOCKING CERVERA AT SANTIAGO.

Reported that Schley's fleet has reached Santiago and is blockading the harbor to prevent the egress of the Spanish fleet. (This report was subsequently confirmed, and a portion of Admiral Sampson's fleet was dispatched to re-enforce Schley. Schley was reported to have declared, "I have seen them (the Spanish fleet) and they will be a long time getting home." The narrow and tortuous nature of the entrance to the Santiago harbor, together with its elaborate fortifications, prevented the United States vessels from entering and giving battle. The entrance was supposed to be thoroughly mined and torpedoed.)

MORAL EFFECT OF MINES.

Anonymous naval authority quoted as saying: "The moral effect of torpedoes and mines will prove far superior to their actual effect. In fact, so great is their moral force that I doubt whether their powers of execution will have an opportunity to be judged in this war."

SUNDAY, MAY 29.
MERRITT'S WIDE LATITUDE.

Full instructions mailed to General Merritt as to the government of the Philippines; instructions reported as giving Merritt fuller discretion than has been given to any Government agent prior to this time.

NO ARMY NEWS.

Censorship of telegraphic communications extended to include all army movements in Florida. Reported that orders have been issued for immediate dispatch of all regular troops of the best prepared volunteers to Cuba and Porto

Rico. (This latter report was contradicted and reasserted persistently during the days immediately succeeding, and nothing definite was known until after the landing of United States troops in Cuba. It was generally understood that the troops were to be convoyed by certain vessels of the fleet of Admiral Sampson.)

A FORTUITOUS NATIONAL POLICY.

Henry Norman, the editorial correspondent of the London Chronicle, declares that inquiry discloses that the administration has not fixed upon a definite policy as to the Philippines or other territorial acquisitions, as the outgrowth of the war; that issue of territorial expansion is entirely unpremeditated and fortuitous, due to the unforeseen necessity of the battle of Manila.

OFFICIAL STEPS TOWARD ANGLO-AMERICAN ALLIANCE.

The London Telegraph declares that preliminary official steps have been taken looking toward the formation of an offensive and defensive Anglo-American alliance, the terms to involve reciprocal support of Great Britain in the Orient and of the United States in the outcome of the Spanish war and in the maintenance of the Monroe doctrine.

MONDAY, MAY 30.
LAND SIEGE TO AID SCHLEY.

Reported that in event of Schley's victory over the Spanish fleet prior to arrival of the army for his assistance, the army will be deflected for immediate invasion of Cuba. (It was proposed to aid Schley in dislodging the Spanish fleet by the establishing of a land siege, aided by heavy siege guns. The expedition to Porto Rico seemed to increase in importance from this time, palpable efforts being made to secure the island, probably to hold for the enforcement of indemnity, before Spain could establish suit for peace.)

MEMORIAL DAY.

Notable participation in Memorial Day observances by the volunteers and by the veterans of both Union and Confederate armies of the Civil War.

TUESDAY, MAY 31.
TRYING THE SANTIAGO GUNS.

Schley's squadron engages the forts at the mouth of Santiago harbor to test calibre and range; finds guns to be heavy and of long range.

Joseph Leiter closes his wheat deal; price of July wheat declines to $1.25 per bushel.

WEDNESDAY, JUNE 1.
SEVENTY THOUSAND FOR CUBA.

Communication from Secretary of War to Congress discloses plan of administration to dispatch expedition of 70,000 men to Cuba.

FRIDAY, JUNE 3.
CASTELAR CHARGED WITH TREASON.

Text of letter of Emilio Castelar in Petit Revue Internationale criticising the Queen Regent for unwarrantable assumption of power in negotiation with the Pope for mediation in the war with the United States published; motion made in the Spanish Cortes for the prosecution of Castelar on a charge of treason.

AN ANGLO-AMERICAN BANQUET.

Eminent Britishers act as hosts of Americans in London at Anglo-American banquet; British speakers praise the American revolutionists and condemn the acts of King George which caused the revolution; desirability of Anglo-American alliance emphasized by all speakers.

SENATE FAVORS BONDS.

Senate, by vote of 45 to 31, adopts minority report on war revenue bill, providing for issue of $100,000,000 certificates of indebtedness, and $300,000,000 of bonds to be used exclusively for war purposes.

HOBSON AND THE MERRIMAC.

Coaling ship Merrimac sunk in the mouth of Santiago harbor by a volunteer crew under naval constructor, Lieutenant Richmond P. Hobson; vessel is sunk to obstruct the harbor and prevent escape of the Spanish fleet, thus relieving a portion of the blockading fleet.

THE NAVY.

NEW ORGANIZATION.

The naval appropriation bill, passed by the 55th Congress, provided for the increase of the number of enlisted men in the navy by 1750, and of the apprentices by 250, enlarging the payroll from $8,235,000 to $9,125,000.

The bill authorized the appointment for temporary service of twenty-five acting assistant surgeons, with rank and pay of assistant surgeons.

The bill established the active list of assistant paymasters at twenty-five.

The bill authorized the construction of three sea-going coastline battleships, to carry the heaviest armor and the most powerful ordnance, with displacement of about 11,000 tons, to have highest practicable speed, and to cost not exceeding $3,000,000 each, one of the ships to be named the Maine.

The bill directed that contracts for the vessels be made within sixty days after the approval of the bill.

The bill also provided that four harbor defense monitors, sixteen torpedo boat destroyers, twelve torpedo boats and one gunboat for the Lakes.

FUNCTIONS OF THE WAR BOARD.

In an interview Secretary Long of the Navy declared as follows:

"The War Board is not a formal body. It has no set rules and regulations, and is not composed of a certain number of men. Its members are officers in whose judgment the Secretary of the Navy has confidence, and they act merely as advisers. The principal function of the Board is to collect information about the enemy and to furnish it to the commanders of American squadrons or single vessels.

"The Secretary of the Navy is not bound by its advice, and there never has been any intention to have the Board determine what Admiral Sampson, for example, should do in certain cases. The Board has means of securing information not accessible to squadron commanders, and it considers all the data and news it receives and transmits them in compact form to the officer or officers to whom they will be valuable."

OFFICERS.

Rear-Admirals—W. A. Kirkland, Joseph N. Miller, Montgomery Sicard (on sick leave and at headquarters), E. O. Matthews, (on sick leave and at headquarters), C. S. Norton, Francis M. Bunce, George Dewey; Acting. W. T. Sampson.

NAVAL BUREAU CHIEFS.
War Board.
Rear-Admiral Montgomery Sicard, president; Captain A. T. Mahan, Captain A. S. Crowinshield.

Retiring Board	Rear-Admiral O. E. Matthews
Bureau of Yards and Docks	Mordecai T. Endicott
Navigation	Captain A. S. Crowinshield
Ordnance	Captain Charles O'Neill
Lighthouse Board	Commodore F. V. McNair
Naval Inteligence	Commodore J. R. Bartlett
Equipment	Commodore R. B. Bradford
Construction and Repair	Philip Hichborn
Steam Engineering	Commodore George W. Melville
Supplies and Accounts	Edwin Stewart
Surgeon-General	Van Reypen

CIVILIAN APPOINTMENTS.
ASSISTANT SURGEONS.

J. Benjamin Dennis, Maryland; Thomas L. Rhoades, Pennsylvania; E. O. Huntington, Minnesota; William S. Thomas, New York; Ralph T. Orvis, California; E. V. Armstrong, New York; W. H. Bucher, Pennsylvania; Edgar Thompson, Missouri; Eugene Grow, New Hampshire.

Assistant Paymasters—Arthur F. Huntington, New York; Harry H. Balthis, Colorado; Charles Conard, New York; William T. Gray, North Carolina; George P. Dyer, New York; A. B. Pierce, Texas; Robert H. Orr, Delaware; Frank W. Hart, District of Columbia; Webb Van H. Rose, New York; Charles W. Penrose, New York; Abel B. Pierce, Texas.

NAVAL COMMANDS.

North Atlantic Squadron—Acting Rear-Admiral W. T. Sampson.
Asiatic Squadron—Rear-Admiral George Dewey.
Pacific Station—Rear-Admiral J. N. Miller.
Flying Squadron—Commodore W. S. Schley.
Northern Patrol Squadron—Commodore John A. Howell.
Naval Base of Supplies—Commodore G. C. Remey.
Coast Defense Fleet—Rear-Admiral Henry Erben.

VESSELS AND GUNS.
(Numerals Indicate Number of Guns.)

Battleships—Iowa, 18; Indiana, 16; Massachusetts, 16; Oregon, 16; Texas, 8. In course of construction—Kearsage, Alabama, Kentucky, Illinois, Wisconsin, Farragut; contracting, three unnamed; total, 14.

Cruisers—Baltimore, 10; Bancroft, 4; Boston, 8; Brooklyn, 20; Charleston, 8; Cincinnati, 11; Columbia, 11; Detroit, 10; Marblehead, 10; Minneapolis, 11; Montgomery, 10; Nashville, 8; Newark, 12; New

Orleans, 6; Newport, 6; New York, 18; Olympia, 14; Raleigh, 11; San Francisco, 12. Total, 19.

Monitors—Amphitrite, 6; Catskill; Comanche; Jason; Lehigh; Miantonomoh, 4; Montauk; Monadnock, 6; Monterey, 4; Nahant; Nantucket; Passaic; Puritan, 10; Terror, 4; Wyandotte. Total, 15.

Gunboats—Annapolis, 6; Bennington, 6; Castine, 8; Concord, 6; Helena, 8; Lancaster; Machias, 8; Marietta, 6; Michigan, 4; Mohican, 10; Monocacy, 6; Petrel, 4; Princeton; Wilmington, 8; Topeka; Vicksburg, 6; Wheeling, 6. Total, 17.

Rams—Katahdin.

Torpedo Boats—Cushing, Dupont, Ericcson, Foote, Gwin, McKee, Morris, Porter, Rodgers, Stiletto, Talbot, Winslow. Total, 12.

Torpedo Boat Destroyer—Bailey.

Dynamite Gun—Vesuvius, Buffalo. Total, 2.

Revenue Cutters—Manning, McCulloch, Gresham, Algonquin (re-named Accomac), Windom, Woodbury, Dexter, Hamilton, Morrill, McLane, Galveston, Forward, Colfax, Boutwell, Winona, Hudson, Calumet, Morrow, Bear, Rush, Perry, Grant, Corwin. Total, 24.

Training Ships—Alliance, 6; Constellation. Total, 2.

Dispatch Boats—Dolphin, Fern.

Receiving Ships—Franklin, 30; Independence; Richmond; Vermont; Wabash, 20. Total, 5.

Special Service—Michigan, 4.

Practice Ships—Monongahela, Pensacola. Total, 2.

RECENT ACQUISITIONS.
(Including Charters.)

Special Board on Inspection and Purchase of Auxiliary Vessels—Captain Frederick Rogers, chairman; Lieutenant-Commander J. D. J. Kelley, adviser; Chief Engineer A. F. Dixon; Assistant Naval Constructor J. C. Towresey; Lieutenant Nathan Sargent, recorder.

Armored Cruisers—Amazonas (re-named New Orleans), 3450 tons; 20 knots; six 6-inch, four 4.7-inch, four 1-pounder rapid-fire guns; two landing guns. Almirante Abrouall (re-named Albany), same as Amazonas.

Gunboats— Diogenes, re-named Topeka.

Torpedo Boats—German Craft, re-named Somers; un-named, christened Manly.

Dynamite Cruiser—Nictheroy, re-named Buffalo.

Auxiliary Cruisers—Paris, re-named Yale; New York, 10,000 tons, re-named Harvard; St. Paul; St. Louis; El Sol, re-named Prairie, 6300 tons, 10 guns; El Norte, re-named Yankee, 6300 tons, 10 guns; El Rio, re-named Yosemite; El Sud, re-named Dixie; Yorktown, re-named Resolute; Venezuela, re-named Panther; Yumuri, re-named Badger.

Yachts—Almy, re-named Eagle; Hermione, re-named Wasp; Columbia, re-named Hawk; Alicia, re-named Hornet; Saturn; Corsair, re-named Gloucester; Sovereign, re-named Scorpion; unknown, re-named Scipto; Thespia; Vixen; Yankton; Hist; Rhaetia, Sauthery, Hannibal.

Tugs—DeWitt C. Ivins, re-named Nezinscott; Winthrop, re-named Osceola; P. H. Wise, re-named Sioux; El Toro, re-named Algonquin; Atlas; Edgar T. Luckenback, re-named Tecumseh; Walter A. Luckenbeck, re-named Uncas; J. D. Jones, re-named Apache; Fearless; Vigilant; Active; Iroquois; Leyden; Potomac; Wompatuck.

Transports—Badger, City of Peking, Panther, Samoset, City of Sydney, Australia, Ohio, Zealandia, China, Colon, Senator.

Colliers—Coaler, Chickasaw, Lebanon, Nanshan, Saturn, Scindia,

Kingtor, Abarenda, Merrimac, Jensen, re-named Brutus; Justin, Leonidas, Iris.

Tenders—Mangrove, Suwanee, Maple, Armeria.

Distilling Boat—Niagara.

Hospital Ships—Creole, re-named Solace; John Englis, re-named Relief.

Refrigerator Ship—Supply.

Supply Ship—Zafiro.

Miscellaneous—Aileen, Alice, Armeria, Atala, Caesar, Celtic, Choctaw, Dorothea, Free Lance, Hercules, Oneida, Peoria, Pompey, Powhatan, Tacoma, Viking, Vulcan, Yangton, Lucerne, Irrawaddy, Yumuri, C. G. Coyle, Penwood, T. P. Fowler, Right Arm, John Doyle, Constance.

NAVAL SQUADRONS.

Atlantic Squadron, W. T. Sampson, Rear-Admiral, commanding—New York (flagship), Iowa, Indiana, Oregon, Miantonomoh, Fern, Amphitrite, Puritan, Terror, Cincinnati, Marblehead, Montgomery, Bancroft, Dolphin, Detroit, Castine, Lancaster, Nashville, Helena, Vicksburg, Wilmington, Newport, Vesuvius, Machias, Foote, Dupont, Ericsson, Stiletto, Cushing, Porter, Rodgers, Winslow, Leyden, Samoset.

Flying Squadron, W. S. Schley, Commodore, commanding—Brooklyn (flagship), Texas, Massachusetts, Iowa, New Orleans.

North Atlantic Patrol, Commander John A. Howell—Ram Katahdin, cruisers San Francisco (flagship), Minneapolis, Columbia; auxiliary cruisers Yankee, Dixie, Prairie, Yosemite.

Mosquito Fleet, Henry Erben, Rear-Admiral, commanding—Consists of auxiliary cruisers, yachts (gunboats) and tugs.

Asiatic Squadron, George Dewey Rear-Admiral, commanding—Olympia (flagship), Baltimore, Boston, Charleston, Raleigh, Concord, Monocacy, Petrel, Nanshan, Zafiro, Monterey.

Pacific Squadron, Joseph N. Miller, Rear-Admiral, commanding—Philadelphia (flagship), Charleston (ordered to Asiatic squadron), Monterey (ordered to Asiatic squadron), Monadnock, Mohican, Comanche, Bennington, Adams, Yorktown, Perry, Grant, Corwin, Rush, Patterson, Hasler, McArthur, Albatross, Alert.

SAMPSON'S FLEET.

New York—Armored cruiser, 8480 tons; 21 knots; six 8-inch, twelve 4-inch rapid-fire, eight 6-pounders, four 1-pounder, four machine guns.

Indiana—Coast line battleship, 10,288 tons; 15.5 knots; four 13-inch, eight 8-inch, four 6-inch, twenty 6-pounder rapid-fire, six 1-pounders, four machine guns.

Oregon—Coast line battleship, 10,288 tons; 15.5 knots; four 13-inch, eight 8-inch, four 6-inch, twenty 6-pounder rapid-fire, six 1-pounders, four machine guns.

Terror—Coast defense monitor, 3990 tons; 10 knots; four 10-inch, two 6-pounder rapid-fire, two 3-pounders, two 1-pounders, two machine guns.

Amphitrite—Coast defense monitor; 10.5 knots; four 10-inch, two 4-inch rapid-fire, two 6-pounders, two 3-pounders, two machine guns.

Detroit—Unarmored cruiser, 200 tons; 18.71 knots; nine 5-inch rapid-fire, six 6-pounders, two 1-pounders, two machine guns.

Montgomery—Unarmored cruiser, 2000 tons; 18.87 knots; nine 5-inch rapid-fire, six 6-pounders, two 1-pounders, two machine guns.

SCHLEY'S SQUADRON.

Brooklyn—Armored cruiser, 8480 tons; 21.9 knots; eight 8-inch, twelve 5-inch rapid-fire; twelve 6-pounders, four 1-pounders; four machine guns.

Iowa—Battleship, 11,296 tons; 16.1 knots; four 12-inch, eight 8-inch, six 4-inch rapid-fire, twenty 6-pounders, six 1-pounder, four machine guns.

Massachusetts—Coast line battleship, 10,288 tons; 16.2 knots; four 13-inch, eight 8-inch, four 6-inch, twenty 6-pounder rapid-fire, six 1-pounders, four machine guns.

Texas—Battleship, 6300 tons; 17 knots; two 12-inch, six 6-inch, twelve 6-pounders rapid-fire, six 1-pounders, four machine guns.

Miantonomoh—Coast defense monitor, 3990 tons; 10.5 knots; four 10-inch, two 6-pounders rapid-fire, two 3-pounders, two 1-pounder guns.

New Orleans—Sheathed cruiser, 3600 tons; 20 knots; six 6-inch, four 4.7-inch, ten 6-pounder and four 1-pounder rapid fire, four machine guns.

THE CUBANS.

CUBAN LEADERS.

Masso, President of the Republic of Cuba; T. Estrada Palma, Delegate to the United States; Maximo Gomez, General-in-Chief of Cuban Army; Calixo Garcia, General in command of Eastern Division of Cuban Army; Gonzalo de Quesada, Secretary of the Cuban Junta in the United States; Horatio Rubens, Counsel to the Cuban Junta.

CUBAN FORCES.

(Estimate of Lieutenant-Colonel Charles Hernandez.)

Under General Gomez—3000 men concentrated; with 6000 men additional at scattered points.

Under General Garcia—Headquarters Bayamo—3000 men; 9000 additional men scattered, and all east of La Trocha.

SPANISH CABINET.

President of the Council of Ministers—Sagasta.
Minister of Foreign Affairs—Duke Almodivar.
Minister of War—Correa.
Minister of Marine—Aunon.
Minister of Colonies—Romero Giron.
Minister of Finance—Lopez Puigcerver.
Minister of the Interior—Capdebon.
Minister of Public Instruction—Gamazo.

A CHRONICLE OF THE WAR.

SPANISH NAVY.

OFFICERS.

Admirals—F. Chacon, ranking officer; Patricio Montijo, Philippine squadron; Camara, Cadiz squadron; Cervera, Cape Verde fleet. Commodore—Villamil, torpedo flotilla.

VESSELS.

Armored—Modern Battleship, Pelayo.

Old-fashioned Battleships—Vitoria and Numancia.

Cruisers—Infanta Maria Teresa, Almirante Oquendo, Vizcaya, Princessa Asturias, Carlos V, Cristobal Colon.

Unarmored—Alfonso XII, Alfonso XIII, Lepanto, Reina Christina*, Reina Mercedes Velasco, Conde Venadito, Don Antonio Ulloa, Don Juan de Austria*, Infanta Isabel*, Isabel II, Ensenada, Isla de Cuba*, Isla de Luzon, Filipinas, Nuevo Espana, Galicia, Marquez de Molino, Martin Alonzo Pinzon, Rapido, Temerario, Vincente Yanez Pinzon, Destructor.

Auxiliary—Spain has thirty-two steamers of the Campania Transatlantica and numerous other merchant vessels, the names of which have not been published.

CAPE VERDE FLEET.

Admiral Cervera, commanding.

Vizcaya—Armored cruiser, 20 knots; 7000 tons; 20 knots; two 11-inch, ten 5.5-inch rapid-fire, two 2.7-inch, eight 2.2-inch four 1.4-inch, two machine guns.

Almirante Oquendo—Armored cruiser, 7000 tons; 20 knots; two 11-inch, ten 5.5-inch Hontorias, ten 5.5-inch, eight 1.4-inch rapid-fire, two machine guns.

Cristobal Colon—Armored cruiser, 6840 tons; 20 knots; two 11-inch Hontorias, ten 5.5-inch Hontorias, eight 2.2-inch rapid-fire, eight 1.4-inch, two machine guns.

Infanta Maria Teresa—Armored cruiser, 7000 tons—Similar to the Vizcaya.

Furor—Torpedo boat, 28 knots; two 14-pounder rapid-fire, two 37 millimeters automatic guns; all guns Maxim-Nordenfelt.

Terror—Torpedo boat—Same as Furor.

Pluton—Torpedo boat destroyer, 30 knots; two 12-pounder two 6-pounder, two 1-pounder guns.

Ariete—Torpedo boat, 26.1 knots.

Azor—Torpedo boat, 24 knots.

Rayo—Torpedo boat, 25 knots.

PRIZES OF WAR.

Prize Court.

John A. Wynne, Commissioner.

G. R. Bowen Patterson, President.

LAW OF DISTRIBUTION.

If the sale of the prize is ordered the gross proceeds are

to be deposited with the Assistant Treasurer of the United States at the place nearest to the sale subject to the orders of the court. The court is to make a decree of distribution determining what vessels are to share in the prize and whether the prize was of superior, equal or inferior force to the vessel or vessels making the capture. The net proceeds of all property condemned as prize shall, when the prize was of superior or equal force to the vessel or vessels making the capture, be decreed to the captors; the proceeds shall, when the prize was of inferior force to the vessel or vessels making the capture, be decreed in one-half to the United States and in the other half to the vessel or vessels making the capture. In cases where the amount in controversy exceeds $2000, appeal may be taken to the Supreme Court.

SPANISH VESSELS CAPTURED.

Date.	Vessel.	Value.	Captor.
April 22	Buena Ventura	$150,000	Nashville.
April 22	Pedro	150,000	New York.
April 23	Mathilde	15,000	Porter.
April 24	Miguel Jover	400,000	Helena.
April 24	Catalina	400,000	Detroit.
April 24	Saturnina (released)	425,000	Winona.
April 24	Sofia	12,000	Porter.
April 24	Saco	....	Terror.
April 24	Canelita	7,000	Wilmington.
April 24	Tres Hermanas	....	Terror.
April 25	Panama	....	Mangrove.
April 26	Paquete	....	Newport.
April 26	Septembre	....	Helena.
April 26	Pireneo	....	Newport.
April 27	Bolivar	....	Terror.
April 27	Guido	400,000	Terror.
April 28	Engracias	....	Newport.
April 28	Lola	....	Dolphin.
April 29	Argonauta (cargo of war supplies)	....	Nashville.
May 1	Masota	....	Foote.
May 2	Paco	....	Newport.
May 5	Oriente (released)	....	Helena.
May 5	Suarez	....	Uncas.
May 6	Frasquito	....	Montgomery.
May 6	Lorenzo	....	Montgomery.
May 7	Espano	....	Newport.
May 7	Padre de Dios	....	Newport.
May 8	Santiago-Apostal	....	Mayflower.
May 9	Fernandeto	....	Vicksburg.
May 9	Severito	....	Dolphin.
May 12	Rita	....	Yale.
May 18	Carlos F. Rosas	....	New York.

AMERICAN VESSELS CAPTURED.

Date.	Vessel.	Value.	Captor.
April 27	Saranac (taken at Iloilo, Phil. Is.)	$40,000	El Cano.

THE CLIMATES.

FEVER IN CUBA.

Reports of Cuban physicians show that 75 per cent of the Spanish soldiers in Cuba suffered with climatic diseases; 50 per cent of these with yellow fever, usually mild; and 25 per cent with malarial fever. Prior to the Cuban war 30 per cent of the foreigners in the island suffered with yellow fever; the mortality among them was 10 per cent.

Cuban physicians unite in stating that improved hygienic methods will greatly reduce the danger from the disease.

Very little yellow fever exists in Cuba in the months of January, February and March; some cases, not many, appear in April, May, June and July, the season during which the current campaign is to be carried on. The rains begin in the middle of August and from that time until the middle of November yellow fever is very prevalent and severe. Foreigners in good physical condition, however, can resist it.

Fever is most prevalent in large towns and near the coast. Six or ten miles from the coast, and at an altitude of 1000 feet, all people are particularly immune.

The most important regulation for soldiers camping in Cuban fields is that the tents must be water-tight, especially impervious to the heavy dews.

Sufferers from the fever usually remain debilitated for about six to ten weeks.

The former United States Consul at Matanzas, A. G. Brice, declares that there is little danger from fever in Cuba if the sanitary rules are properly observed. Mr. Brice maintains that field operations also are practically safe if reasonable sanitary precautions are adhered to.

CLIMATE IN MANILA.

Mr. Joseph E. Stephens, writing in the New York Evening Post from personal observation, said of Manila:

"The city, though low, is, broadly speaking, healthy, except for smallpox, which flourishes unnoticed in the crowded houses of the lower, half-caste natives and Chinese, and malarial typhoid, which chooses the careless foreign resident for its attentions. The black plague has never reached the Philippines, but the cholera used to decimate Manila's native population before a generous benefactor gave the city its present good water supply system. Since then that dread disease has kept away, and the mortality in that center of 350,000 Malays, half-caste Chinese, and Europeans does not probably exceed three per cent per annum.

"In spite of what people who have never been at the Philippines may say the climate of Manila, even in summer, is healthy and free from danger to the white race. American soldiers could want no more salubrious watering place than a camp on the island of Corregidor by which sweep all the fresh breezes that blow from Manila bay and the China sea."

BASIS OF RATIONS.

Each 1000 rations consists of bacon, 750 pounds; hard bread, 1000 pounds; baked beans, 150 pounds; potatoes, 1000 pounds; coffee, roasted, 80 pounds; sugar, 150 pounds; vinegar, 80 pounds; candles, 15 pounds; soap, 40 pounds; salt, 40 pounds; black pepper, 2½ pounds; total net weight, 3307 pounds; gross weight, 3638 pounds.

THE ARMY.

NEW ORGANIZATION.

The Hull reorganization bill provides for an increase of the army to 2348 officers and 104,384 men, distributed as follows.

Cavalry—552 officers; 12,050 men. Artillery—469 officers; 16,457 men. Infantry—1327 officers; 75,125 men. Engineering troops—752 men.

This is an increase over the preceding army establishment of 738 officers and 78,954 men.

The bill allows the President to establish a third battalion for each infantry regiment.

The bill allows increase in company strength to the following totals:
Infantry companies, 250 men; cavalry troops, 100 men; heavy artillery batteries, 200 men; field artillery batteries, 173 men; engineer companies, 150 men.

The bill increases the pay of enlisted men actually serving in commands operating against an enemy 20 per cent. This makes the payment of privates in the current war, $15.60 per month.

OFFICERS.

Major-General Nelson A. Miles, commanding.
Major-General Henry C. Corbin, Adjutant-General.

STAFF OF MAJOR-GENERAL MILES.

Captain Francis Michler, Aid; Captain Marion P. Maus, Aid; Major-General Joseph C. Breckenridge, Chief of Staff; Brig.-Gen. John C. Gilmore, Assistant Adjutant-General; Colonel Charles R. Greenleaf, Assistant Surgeon-General; Lieutenant-Colonel A. L. Wagner, Assistant Adjutant-General; Major Henry B. Osgood, Commissary; Major Eli L. Huggins, Captain Stephen Y. Seyburn, Captain Hugh L. Scott, First Lieutenant Edward Anderson.

BUREAU CHIEFS OF THE ARMY.

Adjutant-General .... Brigadier-General H. C. Corbin
Inspector-General .... Major-General Joseph C. Breckenridge
Judge Advocate-General .... Brigadier-General G. N. Lieber
Quartermaster-General .... Brigadier-General M. T. Ludington
Commissary-General .... Brigadier-General Charles P. Eagan
Surgeon-General .... Brigadier-General George M. Sternberg
Paymaster-General .... Brigadier-General T. H. Stanton
Chief of Engineers .... Brigadier-General John M. Wilson
Chief of Ordnance .... Brigadier-General D. W. Flagler
Chief Signal Officer............... Brigadier-General A. W. Greeley

DEPARTMENT COMMANDERS.

Department of the Pacific—Headquarters, Philippine Islands; Major-General Wesley Merritt, commanding.
Department of the Gulf—Headquarters, Atlanta, Ga.; Major-General J. R. Brooke, commanding.
Department of the East—Headquarters, Governors' Island, N. Y.; Brigadier-General R. T. Frank, commanding.
Department of the Missouri—Headquarters, Omaha, Neb.; Brigadier-General E. V. Sumner, commanding.
Department of Colorado—Headquarters, Denver, Col.; Brigadier-General E. V. Sumner, commanding.
Department of the California—Headquarters, San Francisco, Cal.; Major-General H. C. Merriam, commanding.
Department of the Columbia—Headquarters, Vancouver Barracks, Wash.; Major-General H. C. Merriam, commanding.
Department of the Dakota—Headquarters, St. Paul, Minn.; Brigadier-General J. M. Bacon, commanding.
Department of the Lakes—Headquarters, Chicago, Ill.; Brigadier-General J. M. Bacon, commanding.

MAJOR GENERALS.

Major-Generals—Wesley Merritt, William M. Graham, John J. Coppinger, Henry C. Corbin, John R. Brooke, James F. Wade, William R. Shafter, Joseph C. Breckenridge, Henry C. Merriam.

CIVILIAN APPOINTMENTS.

James H. Wilson, Delaware; Fitzhugh Lee, Virginia; Matthew C. Butler, South Carolina; James C. Wheeler, Alabama; Senator W. J. Sewell, New Jersey (withdrawn.)

BRIGADIER-GENERALS.

Thomas M. Anderson, A. K. Arnold, Simon Snyder, Andrew S. Burt, Royal T. Frank, Sam S. Sumner, Guy V. Henry, Lewis H. Carpenter, John M. Bacon, Henry W. Lawton, Theodore Schwan, A. R. Chaffee, Charles E. Compton, John S. Poland, John C. Bates, H. H. Hawkins, Jacob E. Kent, Frances L. Guenther, John I. Rodgers, S. B. M. Young, Edward B. Williston, George M. Randall, William W. Davis, Alfred E. Bates, Robert H. Hall, Edward V. Sumner, Peter C. Hains, George Gillespie, Marks P. Miller, Jacob Kline, Osward H. Ernst, Lloyd Wheaton, Arthur MacArthur, Henry C. Hasbrouck, John C. Gilmore, Wallace F. Randolph, Joseph P. Sanger, Michael V. Sheridan, John N. Andraws, Robert P. Hughes, John B. Babcock.

CIVILIAN APPOINTMENTS.

Frederick D. Grant, New York; Harrison G. Otis, California; Henry M. Duffield, Michigan; Charles King ("Captain"), Wisconsin; Lucius F. Hubbard, Minnesota; George A. Garrettson, Ohio; William A. Gordon, Georgia; James R. Watts, Texas; William Coats, Alabama; John M. Wiley, Pennsylvania; William A. Bancroft, Massachusetts; William J. McKee, Indiana; Francis V. Green, New York; Charles Fitzsimmons, Illinois; Joseph Hudson, Kansas; Joseph R. Lincoln, Iowa; Nelson Cole, Missouri; Leonard W. Colby, Nebraska; Roy Stone, New York; Henry T. Douglass, Maryland.

ARMY CORPS.

FIRST ARMY CORPS, U. S. A.—Headquarters at Chickamauga; Camp George H. Thomas; Major-General John R. Brooke, commanding.

First Division—Major-General Wilson, commanding. First Brigade—Brigadier-General A. S. Burt, commanding—First Ohio, Third Wisconsin, Fifth Illinois. Second Brigade—Brigadier-General C. E. Compton, commanding—Fourth Ohio, Third Illinois, Fourth Pennsylvania. Third Brigade—Colonel Hulings, commanding—Sixteenth Pennsylvania, Second Wisconsin, One Hundred and Fifty-seventh Indiana.

Second Division—Brigadier-General A. K. Arnold, commanding. First Brigade—Colonel Gardner, commanding—Thirty-first Michigan, Third Pennsylvania, One Hundred and Sixtieth Indiana. Second Brigade—Colonel B. D. Spillman, commanding—First West Virginia, One Hundred and Fifty-eighth Indiana, Sixth Ohio. Third Brigade—Colonel C. A. Van Duse, commanding—Fourteenth Minnesota, Second Ohio, First Pennsylvania.

Third Division—Brigadier-General J. S. C. Bates, commanding. First Brigade—Colonel Bobleter, commanding—First Illinois, Twelfth Minnesota, Fifty-first Pennsylvania. Second Brigade—Colonel William A. Pew, commanding—Twenty-first Kansas, Twelfth New York, Eighth Massachusetts. Third Brigade—Commanding officer not yet named—Ninth Pennsylvania, Second Missouri, First New Hampshire.

SECOND ARMY CORPS—Headquarters at Falls Church, Va.; Camp Alger; Major-General William M. Graham, commanding.

First Division—Brigadier-General Francis L. Guenther, commanding—Includes First New Jersey, Second Ohio, Sixty-fifth New York, Sixth Massachusetts, Eighth Ohio, Eighth, Twelfth and Thirteenth Pennsylvania.

First Brigade—Colonel E. A. Campbell, commanding—Includes First New York, Eleventh Ohio, Sixty-fifth New York.

Second Brigade—Colonel D. J. Foster, commanding—Includes Sixth Illinois, Sixth Massachusetts, Sixth Ohio.

Third Brigade—Colonel H. A. Coursen, commanding—Includes Eighth, Twelfth and Thirteenth Pennsylvania.

Unattached—One hundred and fifty-ninth Indiana, Sixth Pennsylvania and Ninth Ohio.

THIRD ARMY CORPS—Headquarters at Chickamauga; Camp George H. Thomas; Major-General James F. Wade, commanding.

Battalion of Engineers—Companies C and E; Captain James L. Lusk, commanding.

Detachment of Signal Corps—First Lieutenant Frank Greene, commanding.

Cavalry—First Brigade, Brigadier-General S. S. Sumner, commanding—Third Cavalry, Sixth Cavalry, Ninth Cavalry. Second Brigade—Brigadier-General S. B. M. Young, commanding—First Cavalry, Tenth Cavalry.

Light Artillery Brigade—Lieutenant-Colonel W. F. Randolph, commanding—Light Batteries E and K, Third Artillery; A and F, Second Artillery; C and F, Third Artillery; B and F, Fourth Artillery; D and F, Fifth Artillery.

Infantry—First Brigade—Brigadier-General Jacob F. Kent, commanding—Sixth, Tenth, Twenty-second and Twenty-fourth Infantry. Second Brigade—Brigadier-General John S. Poland, commanding—Ninth, Thirteenth, Seventeenth and Twenty-first

Infantry. Third Brigade—Brigadier-General Guy V. Henry, commanding—Eighth, Twelfth, Sixteenth and Twenty-fifth Infantry. Fourth Brigade—Brigadier-General A. R. Chaffee, commanding—First, Second, Fourth and Seventh Infantry.

FOURTH ARMY CORPS, U. S. V.—Headquarters at Mobile—Major-General John J. Coppinger, commanding. (Organization not completed; forces transferred to Tampa on departure of First Corps from that point.)

FIFTH ARMY CORPS, U. S. V.—Headquarters at Tampa—Major-General William R. Shafter, commanding.

First Division—Major-General William R. Shafter, commanding—Includes Sixth, Sixteenth, Tenth, Twenty-first, Thirteenth, Ninth and Twenty-fourth United States Infantry.

Second Division—Brigadier-General A. R. Chaffee, commanding—Includes Eighth and Twenty-second Infantry; Fourth, Twelfth, Twenty-fifth, Seventh and Seventeenth Infantry; volunteers from Massachusetts.

SIXTH ARMY CORPS, U. S. V.—Major-General James H. Wilson, commanding—Headquarters at Chickamauga. (Included in First Corps.)

SEVENTH ARMY CORPS, U. S. V.—Headquarters at Tampa, Fla.—Major-General Fitzhugh Lee, commanding.

First Division—Brigadier-General H. H. Hawkins, commanding—Includes volunteers from Ohio, Georgia, Michigan and Florida.

Second Division—Brigadier-General A. S. Burt, commanding—Includes Illinois, North Carolina, Iowa and Wisconsin volunteers.

DEPARTMENT OF THE PACIFIC—Headquarters at Philippine Islands—Major-General Wesley Merritt, commanding.

Staff—First Lieutenant Lewis H. Strother, Aid; First Lieutenant Harry C. Hale, Aid; First Lieutenant T. Bentley Mott, Aid; Lituenant-Colonel John B. Babcock, Adjutant-General; Major Thomas H. Barry, Assistant Adjutant-General; Colonel Robert P. Hughes, Inspector-General; Lieutenant-Colonel James W. Pape, Chief Quartermaster; Lieutenant-Colonel David L. Brainard, Chief Commissary; Lieutenant-Colonel Henry Lippincott, Chief Surgeon; Major Charles McClure, Paymaster; Major E. H. Crowder, Judge Advocate; Major William A. Simpson, Chief of Artillery; First Lieutenant Charles L. Potter, Engineer Officer; Captain Charles E. Woodruff, Attending Surgeon; Major Richard E. Thompson, Signal Officer.

CAMP MERRITT—Major-General Elwell C. Otis, commanding.

First Brigade—Brigadier-General Miller, commanding—Fourteenth and Twenty-third Infantry, Third Artillery, Fourth Cavalry, one company engineers.

Second Brigade—Brigadier-General F. V. Greene, commanding—Thirteenth Minnesota, Twentieth Kansas, First Idaho, First North Dakota.

Third Brigade—Brigadier-General Charles King, commanding—Tenth Pennsylvania, First Colorado, First Nebraska, First Troop Utah Cavalry, Batteries A and B, Utah Light Artillery.

Fourth Brigade—Brigadier-General H. C. Otis, commanding—Seventh California, First Montana, First South Dakota, First Wyoming.

PHILIPPINE EXPEDITION.

First installment, Brigadier-General T. M. Anderson, commanding—Sailed from San Francisco May 25th as follows:

Via transport City of Peking—First California Volunteers, Colonel J. F. Smith; 49 officers and 973 men; 10 officers and 71 men of the navy.

Via transport City of Sydney—13 officers and 318 men of one battalion of Oregon Volunteers; 9 officers and 300 men of four companies of Fourteenth United States Infantry, and one officer and 50 men of the California Heavy Artillery.

Via transport Australia—Headquarters staff and band and two battalions of Oregon Volunteers, comprising 37 officers and 646 men.

Cruiser Charleston sailed from San Francisco May 21st.

Monitor Monterey and collier Brutus sailed from San Francisco June 7th.

CUBAN EXPEDITION.

Major-General William R. Shafter, commanding. Sailed from Tampa, Fla., at noon of June 8th. Comprised 27,000 men, including sixteen regiments of regular and eleven regiments of volunteer infantry, a battalion of engineers, a detachment of signal corps, five squadrons of cavalry, four batteries of light artillery, and two batteries of heavy artillery.

Regular infantry comprised First, Second, Fourth, Sixth, Seventh, Eighth, Ninth, Tenth, Twelfth, Thirteenth, Sixteenth, Seventeenth, Twenty-first, Twenty-second, Twenty-fourth and Twenty-fifth Regiments.

Volunteer infantry included First New York, Thirty-second Michigan, First and Fifth Ohio, Second New York, First District of Columbia, Fifth Maryland, One Hundred and Fifty-seventh Indiana and Third Pennsylvania.

Expedition was convoyed by the battleship Indiana and the gunboat Helena.

Training ship Bancroft was made headquarters of General Shafter.

SPECIAL REGIMENTS.

First Regiment, United States Volunteer Cavalry, Roosevelt's Rough Riders, Colonel Leonard Wood, commanding.

Second Regiment United States Volunteer Cavalry, Torrey's Terrors, Colonel J. L. Torrey, commanding.

Third Regiment United States Volunteer Cavalry, Grigsby's Gallopers, Colonel Melvin Grigsby, commanding.

Astor Battery, Lieutenant Peyton C. March, commanding; John Jacob Astor, sponsor.

MEDICAL CORPS ASSIGNMENTS.

Brigadier-General George Sternberg, Chief Surgeon; Lieutenant-Colonel Clayton Parkhill, Department of the Pacific, ranking Surgeon of Volunteers; Lieutenant-Colonel Rush Heidekoper, First Army Corps; Lieutenant-Colonel A. C. Girard, Second Army Corps; Lieutenant-Colonel J. R. Hoff, Third Army Corps; Lieutenant-Colonel R. M. O'Reilly, Fourth Army Corps; Lieutenant-Colonel B. F. Pape, Fifth Army Corps; Lieutenant-Colonel Nicholas Senn, Sixth Army Corps; Lieutenant-Colonel L. M. Maus, Seventh Army Corps.

THE VOLUNTEERS.

PHYSICAL DEMANDS OF RECRUITS

Hearing must be normal in both ears.

Vision must not fall below 15.20 in either eye, and not below 20.20 unless it can be made normal by proper glasses.

Color blindness is not a cause for rejection, but must be noted on examination form.

Accepted candidates, if between 17 and 18 years of age, should not fall below 5 feet 3 inches in height and 100 pounds in weight; if between 18 and 19 years, 5 feet 3½ inches in height and 105 pounds in weight; if over 19 years, 5 feet 4 inches in height and 110 pounds in weight.

The weight and chest measurement at expiration should not fall materially below the following standard, which, however, is not to be considered as absolute, and should not be strictly adhered to in case of active boys who are less than 18 years of age:

Height.	Pounds.	Chest.
5 feet 4 inches	118	30 inches.
5 feet 5 inches	120	30½ inches.
5 feet 6 inches	122	31 inches.
5 feet 7 inches	124	31¼ inches.
5 feet 8 inches	128	31¾ inches.
5 feet 9 inches	132	32 inches.
5 feet 10 inches	136	32¼ inches.
5 feet 11 inches	142	32½ inches.
6 feet	148	33 inches.

SOME ARMY SALARIES.

(Add 20 per cent for current war.)

Privates, $13 per month; field musicians, $13; wagoners, $14; artificers, $15; saddlers, $15; corporals, $15; sergeants, $18; first sergeant, $25; saddler sergeant, $22; chief trumpeter of cavalry, $22; principal musician, $22; regimental quartermaster, $23; sergeant-major, $23;

CALL FOR VOLUNTEERS.

QUOTAS OF STATES.

STATES.	RENDEZVOUS.	INFANTRY. Regts. and Battalions.	ARTILLERY. (Batteries.)	CAVALRY. (Regts. and Batteries.)
Alabama	Mobile	2 regts. 1 bat.		
Arkansas	Little Rock	2 regts.		
California	San Francisco	1 regt.	1 light	
Colorado	Denver	2 regts. 2 bat.	4 heavy	
Connecticut	Niantic	1 regt.	1 lgt. 2 hvy.	
Delaware	Wilmington	1 regt.		
Florida	Tampa	1 regt.		
Georgia	Atlanta	2 regts.	2 light	
Illinois	Springfield	7 regts.		1 regt.
Idaho	Boise			2 troops.
Indiana	Indianapolis	4 regts.	2 light	
Iowa	Davenport	3 regts.	2 light	
Kansas	Kansas City	3 regts.		
Kentucky	Louisville	3 regts.		2 troops.
Louisiana	New Orleans	2 regts.		
Maine	Portland	1 regt.	2 heavy	
Maryland	Baltimore	1 regt.	4 heavy	
Massachusetts	Springfield	4 regts.	3 heavy	
Michigan	Detroit	4 regts.		
Minnesota	La Crosse	3 regts.		
Mississippi	Jackson	2 regts.		
Missouri	St. Louis	5 regts.	1 light	
Montana	Ft. Harrison	1 regt.		
Nebraska	Lincoln	2 regts.		
N. Hampshire	Concord	1 regt.		
Nevada	Reno			1 troop.
New Jersey	Jersey City	3 regts.		
New York	Peekskill	12 regts.		2 troops.
N. Carolina	Raleigh	2 regts.	1 heavy	
N. Dakota	Fargo			5 troops,
Ohio	Columbus	6 regts.	4 light	2 squads.
Oregon	Portland	1 regt.		
Pennsylvania	Mt. Gretna	11 regts.	4 heavy	
Rhode Island	Providence	1 regt.		
S. Carolina	Charleston	1 regt. 1 bat.	1 heavy	
S. Dakota	Huron			7 troops.
Tennessee	Nashville	3 regts.		
Texas	Houston	3 regts.		1 regt.
Utah	Ogden		2 light	1 troop.
Vermont	Burlington	1 regt.		
Virginia	Richmond	3 regts.		
Washington	Tacoma	1 regt.		
W. Virginia	Martinsburg	1 regt.		
Wisconsin	Milwaukee	3 regts.		
Wyoming	Cheyenne	1 bat.		1 bat. 1 tr.
Arizona	Phoenix			2 troops.
New Mexico	Albuquerque			4 troops.
Oklahoma	Oklahoma City			1 troop.
Dis. Columbia	Washington	1 bat.		

A CHRONICLE OF THE WAR. 133

STATIONS OF VOLUNTEER ARMY.

Following is an official list of the Volunteer troops mustered in, with stations, names of commanding officers and destination, according to orders up to June 1, 1898:

Alabama—First Regiment (Mobile)—Colonel E. L. Higdon, ordered to Department Gulf.
    Second Regiment—Colonel J. W. Cox, for Reserve and Coast Defense.
Arkansas—First Regiment—Colonel Elias Chandler, Chickamauga.
California—First Regiment—Colonel Joseph F. Smith, Department Pacific.
    Seventh Regiment—Colonel John R. Berry, Department California.
    Second Battalion, United States Volunteer Infantry—Lieutenant-Colonel W. R. Johnston, Department California.
    First Battalion—Major Gus. G. Grant, Department California.
    Second Battalion—Major K. K. Whitmore, Department California.
    Four Heavy Batteries—A, B, C, D—Major Frank S. Rice, Department Pacific.
Colorado—First Regiment—Colonel Irving Hale, Manila; two troops to Chickamauga.
Connecticut—First Regiment—Colonel Charles J. Burdette, report to General Merritt.
    Two Batteries Heavy Artillery report to Commanding General Department East.
Delaware—First Regiment—Colonel Israel P. Wickesham, ordered to Department East.
District of Columbia—First Regiment—Colonel G. H. Harries, Chickamauga, Ga.
Florida—First Regiment—Colonel William F. Williams, report to General Shafter.
Georgia—First Infantry—Colonel Alex. R. Lawton, report to Department Gulf.
    Second Infantry—Colonel Oscar J. Brown, Tampa.
    Light Battery A—Captain C. G. Bradley—Department Gulf.
    Light Battery B—Captain G. P. Walker, Department Gulf.
Idaho—Two Battalions Infantry—Lieutenant-Colonel J. W. Jones, San Francisco.
    Troop I, Cavalry—Captain J. T. Brown.
Illinois—First Infantry—Colonel Henry S. Turner, Chickamauga.
    Second Infantry—Colonel G. M. Moulton, Tampa.
    Light Battery A—Captain Phil Yeager, Chickamauga.
    Third Regiment Volunteers—Colonel Bennett, ordered to Chickamauga.
    Fourth Regiment Volunteers—Colonel C. Andel, Tampa.
    Fifth Regiment Volunteers—Colonel Culver, Chickamauga.
    Sixth Regiment Volunteers—Colonel D. Jack Foster, Washington.
    Seventh Regiment Volunteers—Colonel Marcus Kavanagh, Washington.
    First Cavalry—Colonel E. C. Young, ordered to Chickamauga.
Indiana—One Hundred and Fifty-seventh Regiment—Colonel G. M. Steudebaker, Chickamauga.
    One Hundred and Fifty-ninth Regiment—Colonel J. P. Barnett, Chickamauga, Ga.

One Hundred and Sixtieth Regiment—Colonel George W. Gunder, Chickmauga.
One Hundred and Fifty-eighth Regiment—Colonel H. B. Smith, Chickmauga, Ga.
Twenty-seventh Light Battery—Captain J. B. Curtis, Chickamauga, Ga.
Twenty-eighth Light Battery—Captain W. T. Rande, Chickmauga, Ga.

Iowa—Fiftieth Regiment—Colonel D. V. Jackson, Tampa, Fla.
Fifty-first Regiment—Manila.
Fifty-second Regiment—Colonel W. B. Humphrey, Chickamauga, Ga.
Fifty-ninth Regiment—Chickamauga.

Kansas—Twentieth Regiment—Colonel Fred Funston, Manila.
Twenty-first Regiment—Colonel T. G. Fitch, Chickamauga, Ga.
Twenty-second Regiment—Colonel H. S. Lindsay, Washington.

Kentucky—Second Regiment—Colonel E. H. Gaither, Chickamauga.

Louisiana—First Regiment—Colonel William L. Stevens, Department Gulf.

Maine—First Regiment—Lucius H. Kendall Chickamauga.

Maryland—Fifth Regiment—Colonel R. Dorsey, Coale, Chickamauga.
Two Batteries—Lieutenant-Colonel W. P. Lane, Chickamauga.

Massachusettts—First Regiment—Colonel C. Pfaff, Headquarters and two batteries, Salem, Mass.; two batteries at Clarks Point, Mass.; four batteries at Fort Warren, and one battery each at Gloucester, Marblehead, Nahant and Plum Island, Mass.
Second Infantry—Colonel E. P. Clark, Tampa.
Sixth Regiment—Colonel Charles F. Woodward, Washington.
Eighth Regiment—Colonel W. A. Pew, Chickamauga, Ga.
Ninth Regiment—One battalion under Colonel F. C. Bogan, at Quonset, R. I.; one battalion at Fort Adams, R. I, and two companies at Dutch Island, R. I.

Michigan—Thirty-first Regiment Volunteers—Colonel Cornelius Gardner, Chickamauga.
Thirty-second Regiment Volunteers—Colonel William T. McGurrin, Tampa.
Thirty-third Regiment Volunteers—Colonel Charles L. Boynton, Washington.
Thirty-fourth Regiment Volunteers—Colonel John P. Peterman, Washington.

Minnesota—Twelfth Regiment—Colonel Joseph Bobleter, Chickamauga.
Thirteenth Regiment—Colonel C. McC. Reeve, San Francisco.
Fourteenth Regiment—Colonel Charles A. Van Dusen, Chickamauga.

Missouri—Light Battery A—Captain F. M. Rumbold, Chickamauga.
First Infantry—Colonel Edward Baltdorf, Chickamauga.
Second Infantry—Colonel W. K. Cafee, Chickamauga.
Third Infantry—Colonel G. P. Gross, Washington.
Fourth Infantry—Colonel Joseph A. Cooly, Washington.
Fifth Infantry—Colonel Milton Mone, Chickamauga.

Montana—First Regiment—Colonel H. C. Kessler, San Francisco.
Third United States Volunteer Cavalry—Lieutenant-Colonel Charles F. Lloyd, Chickamauga.
First Troop—Captain D. G. Steers, Chickamauga.
Troop M—Captain J. C. Bond.

A CHRONICLE OF THE WAR. 135

New Hampshire—First Regiment—Colonel R. F. Rolfe, Chickamauga
New York—First Regiment—Colonel T. H. Barker, Department East
   Second Regiment—Colonel E. E. Hardin, Chickamauga, Ga.
   Ninth Regiment—Colonel G. J. Greeen, Chickamauga, Ga.
   Third Regiment—Colonel E. M. Hoffman.
   Twenty-second Regiment—Colonel Franklin Bartlett, Department East.
   Forty-seventh Regiment—Colonel J. T. Eddy, Department East.
   Twelfth Regiment—Colonel R. W. Leonard, Chickamauga, Ga.
   Fourteenth Regiment—Colonel F. D. Grant, Chickamauga, Ga.
   Sixty-fifth Regiment—Colonel Samuel M. Welsh Jr., Camp Alger, Falls Church, Va.
   Seventy-first Regiment—Colonel F. V. Greene, Lakeland, Fla.
   Troop A—Captain Badgley, Camp Alger, Falls Church, Va.
   Troop C—Captain B. C. Clayton, Camp Alger, Falls Church, Va.
   Eighth Regiment—Colonel Henry Chauncey, Chickamauga, Ga.
   Sixty-ninth Regiment—Colonel Edward Duffy, Chickamauga, Ga.
   (Colonels Fred D. Grant and F. W. Greene of the New York Volunteers were subsequently appointed Brigadier-Generals.)
New Jersey—First Regiment—Colonel E. Campbell, Falls Church, Va.
   Third Regiment—Colonel Benjamin A. Lee, Headquarters, and Companies B, F, L and I, Pompton Lakes, N. J., and Companies A, C, D, F, G, H and K, Sandy Hook, N. J.
North Carolina—First Regiment—Colonel J. T. Armfield, Tampa, Fla.
   Seventh Regiment and a Battery—Tampa, Fla.
North Dakota—Two Batteries of Infantry—Lieutenant W. T. Freeman, Philippines.
   Two Troops Cavalry to Chickamauga.
Oregon—Second Regiment—Colonel O. Summers, Manila.
Ohio—First Regiment—Colonel C. B. Hunt, Chickamauga.
   Second Regiment—Colonel J. E. Kuert, Chickamauga, Ga.
   Third Regiment—Colonel C. Anthony, Tampa, Fla.
   Fourth Regiment—Colonel Alonzo Colt, Chickamauga, Ga.
   Fifth Regiment—Colonel C. Kennon, Tampa, Fla.
   Sixth Regiment—Colonel W. V. McMackin, Chickamauga, Ga.
   Seventh Regiment—Colonel A. L. Hamilton, Falls Church, Va.
   Eighth Regiment—Colonel C. N. Hard, Falls Church, Va.
   Ninth Battalion (colored)—Major C. Young, Falls Church, Va.
   First Artillery—Major C. T. Atwell, Chickamauga, Ga.
   Twelfth Regiment—Camp Alger, Falls Church, Va.
   Thirteenth Regiment—Camp Alger, Falls Church, Va.
   First Regiment Cavalry—Lieutenant-Colonel M. W. Day, Chickamauga.
Pennsylvania—First Regiment—Colonel W. B. Bowman, Chickamauga, Ga.
   Second Regiment—Colonel B. Porter, Department East.
   Third Regiment—Colonel Robert Ralston, Chickamauga, Ga.
   Fourth Regiment—Colonel D. B. Case, Chickamauga, Ga.
   Fifth Regiment—Colonel Theodore Birchfield, Chickamauga, Ga.
   Sixth Regiment—Colonel J. W. Shall, Falls Church, Va.
   Eighth Regiment—Colonel T. F. Hoffman, Chickamauga, Ga.
   Ninth Regiment—Colonel C. B. Dougherty, Chickamauga, Ga.
   Tenth Regiment—Colonel A. L. Hawkins, Manila.
   Twelfth Regiment—Colonel J. B. Coryell, Falls Church, Va.
   Thirteenth Regiment—Colonel H. W. Coursin, Falls Church, Va.
   Fourteenth Regiment—Colonel W. J. Glenn, Department East.
   Fifteenth Regiment—Colonel W. A. Kreps, Department East.
   Sixteenth Regiment—Colonel W. A. Hulings, Chickamauga, Ga.

Eighteenth Regiment—Colonel M. Smith, Department East.
   Battery A—Captain B. H. Wakerton, Newport News.
   Battery B—Captain A. E. Hunt, Chickamauga, Ga.
   Battery C—Captain G. Waters, Newport News.
   Sheridan Troop—Captain J. W. Jones, Department East.
   Governor's Troop—Captain Frederick Ott, Department East.
   First Troop—Captain H. Jerome, Department East.
Rhode Island—First Regiment—Colonel C. W. Abbott Jr., Department East.
South Carolina—First Battalion Infantry—Major T. Thomson.
   H Battery—Captain E. Anderson, Department Gulf.
South Dakota—First Regiment—Colonel A. S. Frost, Manila.
Tennessee—Third Regiment Infantry.
   Second Regiment—Colonel Keller Anderson.
   Third Regiment—Colonel Tyffe, Chickamauga.
Texas—First Regiment—Colonel Mabrey, New Orleans, La.
   Second Regiment—Colonel L. M. Oppenheimer, Mobile.
   Third Regiment—Colonel R. P. Smith, report to Gen. Graham.
   First Cavalry—Colonel J. S. Watres, report to General Graham.
Utah—Battery A—Captain R. W. Young San Francisco.
   Troop A—Captain Joseph Caine, Department Pacific.
Vermont—First Regiment—Colonel O. D. Clark, Chickamauga, Ga.
Virginia—Second Regiment—Colonel Baker, Tampa, Fla.
Washington—First Regiment—Colonel J. H. Wholley, Department California.
Wisconsin—First Regiment—Colonel S. P. Shadel, Tampa, Fla.
   Second Regiment—Colonel C. A. Born, Chickamauga, Ga.
   Third Regiment—Colonel M. T. Moore, Chickamauga, Ga.
Wyoming—Battalion Infantry—Major F. M. Foote, Manila.
West Virginia—First Regiment—Colonel D. B. Spillman, Chickamauga, Ga.
The Third Volunteer Cavalry—Colonel M. Grigsby—organized in several Western States, is at Chickamauga, Ga.

MINOR CIVILIAN APPOINTMENTS.

BASIS OF APPOINTMENTS.

President McKinley was quoted in the Army and Navy Journal of May 7th as saying: "I have no further intentions of making appointments from civil life as a reward for party fidelity or social influence. Meritorious service in the field and military experience and ability will be the governing factors in the appointments to be made hereafter."

The President added that he would hold back a number of appointments at his disposal for the purpose of awarding gallant and meritorious service in the field.

CIVILIAN APPOINTMENTS.

Colonels: Laurence D. Tyson, Tennessee; William Young, Utah; Duncan H. Hood, Louisiana.

Lieutenant Colonels: Algernon S. Reeves, Tennessee; George Cole, Connecticut; Theodore Roosevelt, New York.

Majors: Eugene O. Fechel, Michigan; James D. Ferguson, District of Columbia; Edward L. Pinkard, Alabama; Louis Duncan, Maryland; Richard H. Savage, New York.

Captains: M. L. Hellings, Florida; Daniel J. Carr, Connecticut; Carl F. Hartman, New York; William H. Lamar, Maryland; Otto A. Nesmith, California; Howard A. Giddings, Connecticut; John W. McConnell, Illinois; Edward B. Ives, New York.

Inspector Generals, rank of Lieutenant-Colonel: John Jacob Astor, New York; Charles A. Whittier, New York; Curtis Guild Jr., Massachusetts. Rank of Major: F. Creighton Webb, New York; James H. McLeary, Texas; Russell B. Harrison, New York; David Vickers, Idaho.

Chief Surgeons, rank of Lieutenant-Colonel: Nicholas Senn, Illinois; Clayton Parkhill, Colorado; Rush Heidekoper, Pennsylvania; Robert W. Cardwell, Oregon. Rank of Major: Frank S. Bourns, Georgia; John A. G. Woodbury, New York; Lewis Schooler, Iowa; Henry F. White, Minnesota; Charles B. Nancrede, Michigan; Thomas E. Evans, Alabama; R. Emmett Giffin, Nebraska; Thomas C. Wright, Tennessee; George R. Fowler, New York; George Cook, New Hampshire; William H. Daly, Pennsylvania; James M. Jenne, Vermont; James H. Hyssell, Ohio; Leonard B. Almy, Connecticut; Jefferson D. Griffith, Missouri; Edward Boeckmann, Minnesota; Sprague Winchester, Mississippi; Donald McLean, Michigan. Rank of First Lieutenant: Patrick J. McGrath, District of Columbia; Clyde S. Ford, West Virginia.

Brigade Surgeons, with rank of Major: Willis G. Macdonald, Georgia; Charles A. Drake, Georgia; Joseph K. Weaver, Pennsylvania; Charles E. Ruth, Iowa; John W. Bayne, District of Columbia; Milo B. Ward, Missouri; S. C. Graves, Michigan; N. S. Jarvis, New York; William Devine, Massachusetts; John C. Martin, Ohio; P. D. McHaughton, Michigan; S. O. L. Potter, California; George M. Smith, Iowa; Arthur Snowden, Virginia; R. S. Sutton, Pennsylvania; Frank Bruso, New York.

Assistant Adjutant-Generals, rank of Major: Fred Bell, Missouri; Robert L. Brown, West Virginia; Major W. Kimball, New York; Charles J. Goff, West Virginia; Richard J. Fanning, Ohio; K. Kyd Douglass, Maryland; Thomas D. Weebe, Nebraska; Frank S. Polk, New York; Moses Walton Jr., Ohio; J. A. Patten, Iowa; Campbell E. McMichael, Pennsylvania; George H. Hopkins, Michigan; John A. Logan Jr., Illinois; George S. Hobart, New Jersey. Rank of Captain: Theodore S. Botkins, Kansas; Jacob E. Bloom, New York; J. H. White, Virginia; John C. Evans, South Carolina; William McCittrich, California; James A. Colvin, New York; Edward Murphy, New York; James B. Morton, Illinois; Charles R. Miller, Ohio; William Astor Chanler, New York; Irskin Hewett, New York; Walter L. Bonve, Massachusetts; Fred A. Alger, Michigan; William Graves Bates, New York; Frederick J. Kountze, Ohio; Charles H. McGill, Minnesota; August P. Gardner, Massachusetts; George R. Voorhies, Kentucky; William E. Horton, District of Columbia; Lars Anderson, District of Columbia; Sherrell Babcock, New York; W. J. Sewell, New Jersey; James G. Blaine Jr., Maine; W. B. Allison, Iowa; Joseph B. Foraker,

Ohio; P. Bradley Strong, New York; Samuel Belford, Colorado; David Elkins, West Virginia.

Judges Advocate, rank of Lieutenant-Colonel: Andrew C. Gray, Delaware; John A. Hill, Iowa; Charles H. Ribble, New York; Fred A. Hill, Connecticut; Charles L. Jewett, Indiana.

Chief Quartermaster, rank of Lieutenant-Colonel: Avery D. Andrews, New York.

Chief and Assistant Quartermasters, rank of Major: Noble H. Creager, Maryland; Sam R. Jones, Oscar F. Long, Fred Van Schrader, Fred G. Hodgson, Thomas Cruse, William A. Wadsworth, New York. Rank of Captain: Cyril W. King, Iowa; Edward E. Robbins, Pennsylvania; Hiram E. Mitchell, Oregon; John B. Jeffrey, Illinois; William D. Jenkins, Texas; Benjamin Johnson, California; James R. R. Hosmer, New York; William A. Harper, New York; G. H. Holden, Minnesota; H. W. Nicholson, District of Columbia; Thomas H. Cavanaugh, Michigan; Elias H. Parsons, Utah; Edward C. McDowell, Tennessee; Francis M. Schroeder, District of Columbia; Arthur Thompson, New York; Charles M. Auger, California; Frank L. Polk, New York; Walter Allen, Mississippi; Clyde D. Hunt, Vermont; L. V. Williams, Ohio; William K. Alexander, Virginia; William G. Ball, Ohio; George C. Bailey, New York; Edwin F. Barrett, Minnesota; Briton Davis, Texas; Harry S. New, Indiana; Fred Buher, District of Columbia; Haldeman P. Young, New York; Ambrose E. Gonzales, South Carolina; Lloyd Carpenter Griscom, Pennsylvania; John C. Breckenridge, New York; Fred W. Cole, Alabama; W. E. English, Indiana; Giles H. Mendin, Iowa; Chester B. Worthington, Iowa; Charles A. Forrest, District of Columbia.

Engineering Officers, rank of Major: Robert C. Berent, Minnesota; Charles L. Woodbury, Vermont; Edward Merrill, Pennsylvania.

Signal Corps, rank of Captain: John B. Inman, Illinois; Thomas F. Clark, Massachusettts; George R. Gyger, Ohio; Benjamin F. Montgomery, Virginia; George W. Butler, Maine; Frank Lyman Jr., Iowa; Frank L. Martin, California; Frederick T. Leigh, New York; Charles D. Connor, Missouri.

Chief Commissaries, rank of Major: Edmund Beach, Montana; Philip Mothersill, New Mexico; Sam W. Hay, Pennsylvania; William M. Abernethy, Missouri; E. S. Garnett, Arkansas; Robert M. Fitzhugh, Pennsylvania; H. Clayton Mullikin, Maryland; James O. Varnedo, Georgia; James H. Moody, North Carolina; Robert Lee Longstream, Georgia; John D. Block, North Dakota; William M. Grinnell, New York. Rank of Captains: John E. Whitmore, Pennsylvania; Warner Harrison, Ohio; Charles E. Cabell, Virginia; John Dubarry Jr., Pennsylvania; Winslow S. Lincoln, Massachusetts; John Landstreet Jr., Tennessee; A. Richard Thompson Jr., Indiana; Edward Clines, Massachusetts; Dan Van Voorhies, Ohio; Philip M. Lydig, New York; E. B. Fenton, Michigan; Miller R. Downing, Ohio; Sam B. Boats, Ohio; Wilson I. Davenny, Illinois; John F. Jenkins, Wyoming; Fred A. Hyde, New York; Lee Linn, Indiana; J. A. Siemeral, Nebraska; William H. Anderson, Ohio; John W. Lytle, Pennsylvania; George B. McCullom, Tennessee; William A. Tucker, Tennessee; Eben B. Fenton, Michigan; Martin M. Marshall, Iowa; Robert H. Beckham, Texas; Peter C. Deming, New York; Morton J. Henry, Pennsylvania; John Carmichael, Virginia; Moses R. Doyon, Wisconain; Seth M. Millikin, Maine; Oliver P. Smith, Pennsylvania; Salmon F. Dutton, Vermont; Theodore B. Hack'ener, Tennessee; M. M. Marshall, Iowa; Frank K. Lord, New York; John H. Earle, South Carolina; James McCleary, Texas; Thomas C. Catchings, Mississippi; Jay Cooke, Pennsylvania; Joseph A. Coxe, Pennsylvania; Stewart M. Brice, New York; Edward R. Hutchins, Iowa; Orson Pet.yjohn, Illinois; Ralph P. Howell, Iowa; Don A. Dodge, Minnesota; James H. McMillan, Michigan; William Larrabee Jr., Iowa; Joseph B. Handy, Delaware; William C. Daniels, Colorado; Warren C. Fairbanks, Indiana; C. D. Coudert, New York; George W. Pellis, New York; E. W. Hurlburt, Colorado; Charles E. Golden, Wyoming; James C. Grant, Minnesota.

Additional Paymasters: Charles B. Houghton, Connecticut; Fred T. Jones, Ohio; George H. Roy, North Dakota; James D. Harvey, Florida; George D. Sherman, Illinois; D. W. White, New Hampshire; Winfield M. Clark, Pennsylvania; James Canby, Colorado; Louis Knapp, New York; John W. Fogler, Kansas; George E. Pickett, Virginia; Brewster C. Kenyon, California; Edward S. Fowler, New York; William H. Rift, Ohio; John P. Townsend, Missouri; John M. Sears, Tennessee; James W. Dawes, Nebraska; Otto Gecker, Georgia; S. M. C. Hays, Colorado; Beverly W. Coinar, Washington; Robert R. Woods, District of Columbia; William A. Merritt, Maryland; Harrison Robins, Mississippi; William H. Doherty, Massachusetts; Charles Morriss Jr., New York; Frank M. Hammond, Massachusetts; Winfield M. Clark, Pennsylvania; Henry C. Fitzgerald, New York; John Demerit, New York; Timothy D. Kelleher, New York; Dan W. Arnold, Illinois; George Vandegrift, Ohio; George C. Steuart, Georgia; George T. Holloway, New York; Herbert M. Lord, Maine; Sam R. McMillin, Minnesota; George B. Guild, Tennessee; James F. Rusting, New York; William G. Gambrill, Maryland; George F. Downey, Utah; George W. Fishback, Missouri; O'Brien Moore, Texas; B. Bradley Ray, Illinois; William H. Stillwell, Arizona; William B. Rochester, District of Columbia; Robert C. Smith, New York; Seymour Howell, Michigan; Clifford S. Walton, District of Columbia; William H. Schofield, California; Stephen Tambrell Jr., Maryland; William J. Cowden, West Virginia; Moses R. Doyon, Wisconsin; F. M. Rix, Arkansas; F. G. Monaghan, Ohio; M. B. Curry, Georgia; James B. Kenner, Indiana; J. S. Wilkins, District of Columbia; M. F. Sheary, New York; Fred Boswick, New York; C. A. Smylie, New York; S. S. Harvey, Florida.

THE CALIFORNIA VOLUNTEERS.

FIRST REGIMENT.

James F. Smith .... Colonel Commanding
Victor D. Duboce .... Lieutenant-Colonel
Charles Baxton .... Major
Charles L. Tilden .... Major
Hugh T. Sime .... Major
Alfred J. Kelleher .... Captain and Adjutant
John J. West .... First Lieutenant and Battalion Adjutant
Fred W. Dohrmann .... First Lieutenant and Quartermaster
Herman Huber .... First Lieutenant and Commissary
William H. Tobin .... First Lieutenant and S. R. P.
Otto Schwerdtleger .... Sergeant-Major
Martin H. Wilkins .... Quartermaster Sergeant
Percy L. Badt .... Battalion Sergeant-Major

COMPANY A—SAN FRANCISCO

Captain John F. Connolly; Lieutenants—George T Ballinger, Joseph A. Brown; Sergeants—Frank McCarthy, Morris Justh; Corporals—Charles L. O'Donnell, Warren F. Lieb, James J. Loughrey, Daniel M. Ritchie; Musicianes—Julius Aitken, Frank S. Wyatt; Privates—John J. Brady, Frederick Bertrand, Daniel Boyle, John J. Campbell, David A. Cutting, M. Cunningham, H. R. Crow, J. A. Dewitt, W. H. Dusenberry, F. Donegan, E. J. Doherty, F. Fiegnero, G. H. Fuerst, Elmer Gabrielson, Max Horn, D. Holland, Nils H. Johnson, W. F. Kays, S. Kats, J. Kilemade, J. J. Lucitt, Alex S. Less, Thomas Lind, J. J. Morris, J. Murphy, Morris L. Markowitz, Edward T. McCaffrey, Frank J. Murphy, Joseph Murdock, W. Ray, J. Riley, Leonard J. Schlink, Louis D. St. Amont, Joseph G. Smith, J. Verheyen, John E. Webster, John Weidlun.

COMPANY B—SAN FRANCISCO—

Captain George Filmer; Lieutenants—B. B. Sturdivant, A. F. Ramm; Sergeants—W. N. Kelly, A. H. Clifford, H. B.

Taylor, H. B. Sullivan; Corporals—C. Lemon, C. Lindecker; Musicians—A. E. P. Apthorpe, W. Proll, D. J. Baird; Privates—D. S. Briggs, W. J. Buttgenbach, L. J. Behin, A. Burtchell, D. Campbell, H. Crowley, A. W. Clark, A. W. Cills, E. O. Cills, G. Cunningham, R. L. Drake, J. V. Dunmore, W. W. Davidson, H. A. Evens, W. G. England, W. C. Eisenschimel, W. B. Eichbaum, P. Eagen, E. L. Filmer, A. H. French, A. C. Fisher, E. V. Fitzgerald, L. F. Freestrom, J. Fisk, W. E. Garrison, J. M. Gove, J. P. Gaffney, A. F. Hammerson, W. J. Hayes, E. W. Hewson, F. H. Holcombe, C. A. Hunter, L. L. Helliwell, L. L. Hunter, T. C. Healion, F. H. Hoyt, E. A. Joy, E. W. Jensen, H. D. Jones, E. Kavanaugh, S. W. Knottner, A. Kuhlman, C. D. Lowe, G. F. Larney, F. M. McCarthy, P. D. McCarthy, J. W. Miller, A. J. Nicholson, G. H. Perkins, S. L. Rodgers, L. G. Russell, W. K. Reed, H. Ruff, T. J. Robinson, C. P. Richardson, S. P. Russell, H. F. Ruthraff, Lloyd Spencer, T. J. Sheehan, L. B. Simon, A. B. Schell, G. G. Spooner, —. Simpson, H. D. Skellinger, W. H. Tooker, J. A. Thompson, W. B. Thompson, A. Wistrand, E. L. Worth, P. A. Williams, E. S. Warton, L. B. Wood, M. D. Zann.

COMPANY C—SAN FRANCISCO—

Captain J. W. Dumbrell; Lieutenants—Charles E. Goodell, George J. Petty; Sergeants—H. T. Hicks, J. Gillis, J. N. Ross, D. E. Lawton; Corporals—J. R. Switzer, W. F. Unfred, A. Frederick; Musicians—John Donald, John S. Crawford, F. F. Carson; Privates—Walter Brind, J. R. Barriclo, W. R. Butler, L. E. Bunner, F. L. Doeing, A. H. English, H. W. Fawke, J. F. Finlay, Alfred L. Franks, Ray L. Huesch, F. W. Held, I. J. Kane, Donald F. McMullan, C. J. McDonald, O. C. Nelson, A. B. Nelson, William E. Roberts, Herbert G. Stewart, W. H. Shaw, C. A. Smith, E. Williams.

COMPANY D—SAN FRANCISCO—

Captain T. J. McCreagh; Lieutenants—Charles G. White, Harry F. McGerren; Sergeants—G. W. Swan, W. D. Flynn, R. B. Downie; Corporals—James F. McCarthy, James O. Staples; Musicians—Walter P. Fisher, Kirke Sampson; Privates—Eugene Aherne, Charles J. Anderson, Charles P. Ayton, J. D. Browne, William T. Baldwin, William J. Beran, Ralph H. Blevin, Richard C. Bolts, William J. Boyer, Mitchell J. Brown, Otto W. Burnett, Elmer F. Butzer, George W. Cole, Edward D. Crowley, Clayton D. Cunningham, Frank S. Cutler, George W. Daly, William H. Daly, Harry B. Dalmas, Charles N. Davis, Isador Davis, Hugh Dempsey, Charles H. Dunfee, Richard P. Farrel, William Foley, Arthur L. Galvin, Thomas J. Galvin, Alfred E. Haggman, Henry F. Haze, J. Koneman, E. C. Kessler, William A. Jameson, Olinto Landucci, John C. Lippert, John J. Loftus, George J. Luttrell, Charles G. Mallon, N. J. Malville, Samuel I. Marston, James W. Master, George J. Mayer, David McKee, F. J. McAllister, James McQueeney, Frank A. Moore, Owen H. Moore, O. Olanducci, James O'Leary, Leon Pauchon, H. D. Pohlman, Thomas R. Pfoff, Henry R. Pfuhl, William T. Phillips, Fred J. Price, W. J. Quirk, Hugo Rosebery, Joseph Rotnman, Walter J. Roussell, Willis A. Rowe, Charles Schrader, Joseph J. Shaw, August A. Sollman, Gabriel Stephens Jr., Harry Swarts, William E. Tucker,

Joseph J. Torrey, William H. Watson, Frank W. West, Louis E. Westphal, John A. Williams, John C. Wulbern, James J. Watkins, Charles Vail.

COMPANY E—SAN FRANCISCO—

Captain, W. R. Robertson; First Lieutenant, J. H. Jordan; Second Lieutenant, Otto Schwerdtfeger; Sergeants—T. Howard, J. Cardiff, M. D. Delaney; Corporals—M. O'Connell, L. E. Twomey, W. E. Wehser, J. Brady, John J. Canavan, John Eagan; Privates—D. Arling, William Cadigan, George Dougherty, M. Dwyer, E. Garry, W. J. Hogan, E. S. Howes, B. F. Jackman, S. P. Jones, J. F. Kane, James Kelley, R. A. Kappen, W. V. Martin, J. L. Morris, F. Mullen, J. Murphy, J. Nolan, E. F. O'Brien, E. J. O'Neill, T. C. Pedlar, J. Rocks, D. M. Ross, T. Sullivan.

COMPANY F—SAN FRANCISCO—

Captain, J. A. Miller; First Lieutenant, A. F. Nippert; Second Lieutenant, Frederick L. Brown; First Sergeant, G. W. Iverson; Quartermaster-Sergeant, C. D. Cook; Sergeants—B. Hawks, B. H. Hawks, H. Turton, H. W. Doscher; Corporals—J. G. Hawks, W. M. Higgins, H. D. O'Brien, A. H. Irving, W. A. Varney, P. H. Raine; Musician, W. G. Berry; Privates—E. R. Ayers, A. DeW. Allen, C. P. Bernal, M. J. Bernal, F. W. Best, J. F. Bickford, W. B. Brown, A. R. Babcock, W. J. Clark, W. Cook, G. T. Colmesnial, W. Cohn, C. S. Cleveland, G. R. Culver, R. J. Cutler, G. E. Crump, E. F. Du Fresne, A. P. Dever, E. F. Duffey, F. H. Field, C. J. Fallon, O. H. Fernback, F. W. Field, J. T. Finnigan, C. L. Girard, G. Gemballa, W. H. Hogue, W. S. Haubridge, E. R. Holsten, P. C. Harlan, J. S. Hall, A. M. Jones, S. A. Newman, M. A. Nathan, C. J. O'Connor, R. C. Jantzen, F. A. Louis, U. C. Meyers, L. C. Miller, W. T. Moran, Frank Meyers, R. H. Norton, C. W. Osborne, D. J. Oliver, G. Ohlsen, G. Peters, T. C. Raymond, C. H. Rockwitz, H. C. Reed, J. Rose, E. E. Surryline, V. H. Sutton, J. L. Simmons, F. J. Suhling, H. A. Stube, H. D. Sydney, C. R. Tinsley, George W. Upp, Julius Witzel, Charles C. Wilmans.

COMPANY G—SAN FRANCISCO—

Captain, E. E. Sutliffe; Lieutenants—T. W. Sparrowe, W. N. Swasey; Sergeants—J. F. Norton, R. J. Dowdall, P. J. Neuman; Corporals—C. P. Hirst, G. W. Simmie, H. H. Morris; Musicians—Francis J. Barry, Leon J. Pelle; Privates—T. G. Bautz, James M. Dabney, J. P. Heilbroun, B. Hopkins, W. H. Norman, R. J. O'Connor, C. E. Thompson, Albert B. Anderson, Franklin W. Aust, Duane Barnes, Louis H. Barieau, John L. Darnes, Arthur S. Hatfield, George W. G. Jackson, Dixon L. Lee, William Menzel, Alex, Martin, Joseph T. McEvoy, M. J. Noonan, John W. Renton, William G. Sparrowe, William D. Stewart, William T. Sullivan, Maurice J. Scanlan, Wilford M. Taylor, William M. Welch, E. A. Colvin, Joseph McAvoy, —. McNally.

COMPANY H—SAN FRANCISCO—

Captain, Frank W. Warren; Lieutenants—Ed. F. Davis, T. P.

O'Brien; Sergeants—A. Ehrenpfort, John E. Broderick; Corporals—
G. E. Hirsinger, L. F. Guedet, Carl Schneider, John J. Binet, Thomas
F. Donovan, Frederick A. Jaggic; Privates—F. Andrews, H. W. Blake,
W. A. Dineen, C. G. Dean, G. L. Field, G. H. Grimes J. J. Kirby, F. C.
Miller, F. Nicholas, R. W. Ruston, J. L. Swift, C. Weckerle, Frank
Angelovich, Thomas T. Bryan, Alfred E. Baker, John J. Blake, George
H. Belmont, Thomas Connor, Joseph F. Conlon, Thomas A. Campbell,
Clarence J. Case, Peter M. Conlon, Frederick L. Crosby, William F.
Dunne, T. A. Dodini, David Fairbanks, William Grady, John J. Greenwood, Theodore L. Holzhausen, F. L. Jackson, John C. F. Koshmitzki,
T. J. Kenny, Frank X. Larkey, Warren D. Lattimer, Frank A. Lawler,
George H. McGinerty, James A. Mulaly, Frank McArdle, A. J. McGee,
Joseph Neilan, Dan J. Nicolls, Joseph A. O'Donnell, Edward A. O'Neill,
John Pierson, Charles F. Raye, George A. Reid, John A. Reach, John
Rourke, George W. Robe, Walter B. Sedgley, Charles H. Smith, Edward Valento, Emil A. Weins, Francis Warren, William Walsh, Henry
F. Young.

COMPANY I—SAN FRANCISCO—

Captain, Reinhold Richter; Lieutenants—O. F. Huber, Frank K.
Moore; Sergeants—Henry Lemeteyere, M. J. Sheahan, William Golly,
Henry Stotzenwald; Corporals—Clarence A. Son, Henry Bucking, H.
G. Mathewson, John G. Cappleman, S. J. Gillis; Musicians, John J.
Van Staden, Cornelius Ryan; Privates—George Balleu, Thomas E.
Allen, H. W. Ayers, John E. Balke, Alex Bernard, H. J. Blackman,
William T. Bogert, E. M. Boysan, B. F. Budd, Josiah L. Carr, Joshua
W. Carr, Henry Castagnino, Americo Chilini, Edward Connell, L.
Crane, John A. Daly, Albert G. Dietrick, J. J. Dremmerand, W. H.
Faxan, John T. Flynn, James R. Franklin, Joseph Fritz, F. E. Funge,
F. L. Funze, Charles C. Garfield, Eugene Geary, A. H. Green, John F.
Hale, James F. Halsey, Harry Hall, W. R. Hanna, McPherson Harrison, Philip Heinz, Fred E. Hoar, Frederick H. Just, Charles Lambe,
John H. Liddle, Robert Luhn, William Lundy, James I. Mackin, Frank
W. Manning, H. F. McSorley, J. M. Murtha, George W. Nepp, George
B. Newberry, R. W. Nicholson, James E. Norton, Daniel O'Neil, Harry
C. Payson, Corwin S. Perry, Michael Quill, P. T. Randi, Elijah Redell,
John C. Reitz, John Rescho, George Rosenberg, Tor. Rosemlund,
Ignitius Salituri, William A. Schmitz, John Shay, George Sheldon,
George D. Siebertt, Charles E. Stuart, G. E. Williams, Thomas Winship, Charles H. Wiseman, William Young.

COMPANY K—SAN FRANCISCO—

Captain, T. J. Cunningham; First Lieutenant, E. D. Finley; Second
Lieutenant, C. W. Seely; Quartermaster Sergeant, J. Bergman; Sergeant, A. R. Farless; Corporals—H. Myers, H. L. Detrick; Musicians—
H. N. Craig, H. J. Wilson; Privates—E. Barnes, W. K. Bush, J. M.
Cassidy, W. J. Daley, J. A. Devany, R. S. Green, E. L. Green, B. D.
Hoffman, M. R. Holling, A. J. Hynes, P. J. Kelly, W. E. Kemp, P.
Kurtz, L. J. Mayer, C. J. Mund, E. M. O'Reilly, E. Stamper, B. P. Walls,
F. E. Young, A. T. Alcott, Clarence F. Alwill, William H. Bessac,
George S. Brooks, Herbert M. Brace, William P. Callahan, James Connoly, Thomas J. Conway, F. A. Corbusier, Emanuel De Sausa, Charles
R. Detrick, Thomas F. Dean, Robert W. Dodd, Alfred R. Dole, Joseph
Dovovan, Malcolm Elliott, William E. Ellis, Elmer W. Emmett, John

A. Fegan, Emmett M. Fowler, Harvey Fry, Edward E. Graw, Roy E. Guidery, John P. Harkins, Robert W. Hartwell, James E. Hicks, William W. Holling, Henry Keiser, James C. Kane, Philip C. Kern, Harry H. Kluie, George F. Knacke, Joseph J. Katinger, Granville E. Leavitt, William Lee, George Lull, Joseph H. Livisey, Arthur F. Lundberg, Thomas F. Nowlan, Harold G. Parks, William E. Perryman, William D. Potter, George L. Rees, Arthur T. Roper, Justin H. Stewart, John R. Stowe, John R. Switzer, Chester A. Thomas, Ernest F. Townsend, Frank N. Turton, Jeremiah Turpin, Robert Westcott, Will R. White, Clarence M. Wardace, Emil Wetheral, William Weider, William A. Wrigley.

COMPANY L—SAN FRANCISCO—

Captain, John F. Eggert; First Lieutenant, Henry E. Curzons; Second Lieutenant, Albert C. Adler; Sergeants—F. J. Grundman, J. M. Foley; Corporals—H. G. Leffmann, H. G. Coleman, Julian Kraimer, Theodore Kruse; Musicians—H. Gordon, E. H. Sengstack; Privates—R. K. Davis, P. J. Finn, E. J. Leary, J. C. Lauber, T. A. Marlowe, H. J. Mangels, F. L. Noriega, F. C. Owens, W. B. Porter, D. I. Rogers, H. G. Rreese, E. Abrams, H. J. Anderson, C. B. Addington, L. Burchard, H. Bittell, A. Buhl, F. S. Brown, P. G. Broad, B. M. Clancey, C. W. Clifton, H. J. Collins, T. F. Collins, G. Donovan, —. Deckleman, J. Donelly, A. H. Daly, G. C. Eldridge, W. J. Eaton, R. B. Ellis, —. Fiske, W. J. Furry, E. E. Grogean, F. C. Haley, F. A. Healey, L. J. Harrison, P. Hiatt, M. R. Kruse, J. C. Klesow, H. J. F. Leffenan, M. T. Loftus, A. J. Lacroix, F. H. Loucke, A. W. Loftus, L. Laurenson, A. Meyer, G. A. Marshall, P. McLaughlin, W. F. Miller, L. Morris, R. R. McGregor, D. McKenzie, J. E. Munster, J. G. McGlynn, C. J. Molke, G. M. C. Nelson, F. W. Neil, J. L. Osborn, Don Prior, J. W. Parnow, H. Ryan, R. A. Stanton, E. D. Schoppe, W. H. Van Hofen, S. Widdifield, J. H. Wohltman, C. J. Wohlers, J. C. White, A. Wigand, E. Wittiman, W. H. Wheeler, H. P. Yerg.

COMPANY M—SAN FRANCISCO—

Captain, Thomas F. O'Neil; Lieutenant, C. J. Hogan; Sergeants—E. W. Rivers, W. L. Wall, William P. Maher; Corporals—E. C. Stroth, J. W. Maher, C. E. Noyes, F. L. Kelly, C. G. Kiey, M. S. McNeil, T. F. Maher, T. Graves; Musician, Albert Ames; Privates—A. J. Bogan, M. S. Bradley, J. C. Corcoran, D. J. Curley, P. H. Fisher, G. H. Fay, Charles E. Johnson, F. J. Kerrigan, F. W. McDonald, A. F. Meinhardt, W. O'Donnell, F. L. Owens, T. P. O'Brien, T. J. O'Neil, A. Pinkert, J. J. Reardan, J. P. Sheridan, J. M. Smith, O. G. Volkman, John H. Boyle, Herbert L. Barrows, Harry A. Baily, James J. Borree, Nelson B. Borree, Oscar Basney, Patrick J. Bartlett, Stephen Burdell, Thomas J. Belton, Richard Collopy, John J. Clancy, E. C. Duwer, William L. Daley, Joseph Downey, Dan J. Gorman, Louis Graham, Ellis B. Holmes, Dennis J. Kelly, Michael J. Lyons, Almy A. Lawton, Paul Langer, E. Mervin, Thomas Michaelson, John M. Miller, Jacob J. Mahr, Hugh P. McSwegan, Matthew F. McHugh, Frank W. Newbert, Frank C. O'Neill, Charles A. Pracht, Frank Paulson, Frank Prideaux, John L. Quinn, Thomas J. Rock, Andrew J. Reilly, James H. Ravekas, James T. Shaw, Charles T. Squire, John Sheill, Addison M. Stringer Jr., Arthur G. Sutherland Jr., Edgar A. Taylor, David B. Taylor, Alfred G. Waller, Carlton F. Whitton, John S. Wheeler.

SIXTH REGIMENT.

W. R. Johnson .... Lieutenant-Colonel, commanding
Gus G. Grant .... Major
R. K. Whitmore .... Major
W. G. Dozier .... First Lieutenant and Battalion Adjutant
  Acting Quartermaster and Commissary..
Thomas W. Johns ....First Lieutenant and Battalion Adjutant
  Acting Regimental Adjutant and Ordnance Officer.

COMPANY A—STOCKTON—

Captain, C. H. Dasher; Lieutenants—G. L. Doll, J. P. Morrell; Sergeants—R. D. Wallam, R. W. Bonney, H. Kroeckel, Charles E. Woods, A. S. Edwards, A. M. Doll; Corporals—F. A. Spence, C. L. Canfield, C. B. Manges, A. H. Jameson, J. E. Lindsay, H. A. Caldwell. Privates—W. F. Anderson, W. Alger, B. Barden, A. J. Berryman, F. H. Blackman, J. S. Bryan, W. Capps, A. Carr, W. T. Cates, F. Coon, W. P. De Carlie, H. C. Denny, George Dewel, A. L. Englehart, S. B. Endicott, C. F. Fruit, H. Gebhardt, M. F. Gebhardt, J. B. Goodwin, F. Grabill, I. A. Grabill, J. Green, W. Gunning, A. H. Hall, A. Hewlett, W. F. Hitchcock, C. J. Howell, P. Jensen, C. E. Keebler, E. W. Kellogg, K. L. Knight, W. E. Matthews, S. McDonough, J. E. McMullen, E. H. Mulveny, L. B. McCoy, I. H. Noble, G. S. Ownings, A. Parsons, H. M. Pembroke, Oscar P. Pile, Charles F. Ramsey, Lee Riley, L. Rhodes, F. W. Reed, W. F. Rodgers, F. J. Scanlan, R. Stowell, T. R. Tuttle, H. C. Utt, W. Von Detten, W. Wells, G. Wagner, W. W. Wood, M. O. Wood, H. H. Wilhelm, A. White, H. D. Lang, W. Hutchinson, H. C. Williams, S. McCurdy, W. T. Jenkins, G. Thurman, Edward Hardy, G. H. Korner.

COMPANY B—STOCKTON—

Captain, William Bruce; Lieutenants—L. A. Eaton, J. Parnan; Sergeants—C. M. Peters, F. A. Elliott, W. E. Laurie, F. R. Gibson, J. W. Bram, C. E. Korell; Corporals—W. A. Hedge, W. Hendershot, W. M. Lanigan, N. J. Vizelich, H. J. Porter, George W. Lockhead; Musicians—A. P. Giovanassi, William R. Diffendorfer; Privates—G. W. Archibald, W. H. Aldridge, E. Anthony, R. A. Beard, G. Batting, H. W. Chase, P. Clarity, A. H. Clyma, F. W. Confer, A. M. Dangle, John Dougherty, John B. Duffey, William F. Dwyer, Charles Donanovich, R. K. Edwards, J. E. Edwards, C. E. Elliott, R. H. English, C. Fisher, A. Fisher, J. E. Gilbert, T. J. Gilbert, A. H. Gocke, E. S. Hickman, R. J. Hildum, H. L. Hite, J. Jurgenson, H. G. King, E. J. Kirwin, William Layton, M. Lesnenni, E. Lewis, A. R. Lombard, J. McGee, A. I. Miller, G. R. Morse, S. R. McKay, M. G. Neto, G. O. Newcomb, I. E. Norris, L. Ososki, L. Palmer, B. Parmer, S. Peri, G. A. Pile, T. D. Portor, F. Pottle, K. Reynolds, S. L. Shook, E. R. Strother, H. Swank, W.

A. Tate, J. A. Triest, M. O. Trobaugh, J. F. Troutman, Harry L. Tuttle, A. C. Ward, T. Ward, J. Wyatt, M. M. Packer, H. H. Siebe, G. C. Cleveland, J. J. Kenney.

COMPANY C—FRESNO—

Captain, George O. Duncan; Lieutenants—J. D. Jones, Edward Jones; Sergeants—J. A. Develin, F. E. Norton, Edward Magee, W. Ferguson, F. M. Holaday, W. S. Scott; Corporals—Charles A. Brutsch, George L. Traber, F. W. Watkins, M. O. Rogers, Edward G. Wright, Alfred Jagger; Musicians—F. J. Knowlock, C. M. Noyes; Privates—Andrew Anderson, William Anderson, A. L. Akers, L. M. Abrogast, E. L. Albin, L. P. Annaux, J. W. Bradford, D. W. Blakey, David Baker, L. L. Babcock, F. F. Bartlett, T. N. Barrett, M. K. Bennett, F. W. Clark, N. B. Converse, R. F. Chapman, F. F. Detoy, N. F. Densmore, L. S. Dennick, H. J. Fairbank, David Forbes, F. G. Forgey, W. J. Faber, Gordon C. Griffin, Will P. Green, John E. Gates, Elmer Gates, John Gray, J. A. Hutchinson, F. G. Hodgkinson, Will L. Hills, W. A. Hutchinson, Will Kelly, W. A. Katsch, Charles H. Ledsinger, C. H. Lawson, F. C. Lofthouse, Charles E. Morss, Lot. L. Mitchell, Henry H. Mills, Robert North, Joseph Phelps, D. E. Robinson, J. W. Rogers, John Roberts, Jesse E. Roberts, Edward B. Russell, A. J. Scott, W. B. Scott, L. L. Scott, D. H. Spence, E. H. Shell, — Smutz, George A. Sullivan, L. F. Thorn, E. R. Twede, James G. Wofford, O. C. Wilcox, F. P. Wills, George H. Wills, Hiram E. Williams, J. G. Wintemute, Charles E. Whitney, A. E. Woodard, H. T. Hutchinson.

COMPANY D—MODESTO—

Captain, D. W. Morris; Lieutenants—G. H. Freitas, H. L. Walthall; Sergeants—W. E. Stuart, C. A. Hanson, R. S. Powell, J. L. Conrad, G. H. Ingle, J. R. James; Corporals—W. H. Fawcett, F. W. Webb, A. L. Hamlin, R. L. Wade, G. B. Leet, C. F. Zander; Musician, W. Bury; Privates—A. J. Albright, W. H. Arnold, F. Bradley, J. Bolnard, W. J. Bell, T. O. Brasher, P. Bowen, F. M. Carsom, C. F. Call, W. C. Christeen, W. Duchran, W. Estes, C. Foster, C. Gardner, W. Harris, W. Hofman, O. Jensen, R. Kattestart, F. Kane, F. Lees, E. Luttrell, H. Martin, F. Marsher, W. Masterson, W. Mavey, E. McDowell, F. McDaniel, E. Muller, W. Oxendine, J. O'Neill, J. Porter, C. Prewett, E. Rinehart, J. Rhea, M. Rasmussen, C. Robertson, W. Robertson, J. Rafter, A. Rose, R. Reeves, E. Randall, F. Smith, E. Silsby, T. Smith, E. Sperry, M. Smith, A. Stolper, L. Serrano, W. Survice, B. Settle, T. Steinberger, C. Sellman, I. Stanley, C. Scott, H. Travers, G. Tharp, J. Tombs, N. Ullom, A. Walker, J. Williams, F. Wilson, I. Webster, C. Witt, A. Woodsen, W. Whitlock, C. Wrightson, T. S. Wilson, D. Nolan.

COMPANY E—VISALIA—

Elder, G. O. Griggs, J. E. Linnell, E. Linnell, Fred Morrison, Ed P. Myers, George Powell, Charles D. Smith, Thomas J. Steinkelner, F. A. Thomas, J. P. Wilkinson, I. E. Abbott, L. Anderson, C. C. Atwell, James Bacon, N. Baker, Charles B. Barlow, F. E. Benn, I. R. Bliss, William F. Brown, C. E. Bryant, R. H. Britton, Kit Carson, C. E. Cole, Charles H. Cornelius, J. G. Danielson, G. H. DeWolf, T. D. Depew, R. A. Drais, James E. Donnelly, G. Earnhart, M. L. Fleming, James E. Finnerty, William K. Ficklin, A. H. Garrison, O. H. Hafley, F. P. Hagler, Oscar Harlan, Gustave Hennis, E. C. Jones, George P. Jordans, Charles B. Koontz, Thomas P. L. Lloyd, Charles A. Myers, H. B. Newman, A. St. J. Oliver, Charles S. Peabody, George Phebus, F. W. Reed, S. E. Rice, John F. Russell, Charles Schleifer, B. F. Sherman, N. H. Soogian, F. A. Townsend, W. J. Traejer, R. S. Wiggin, James A. Wiley, John H. Woodard, George Young, A. R. Shippey, Robert Willson.

COMPANY F—FRESNO—

Captain, John F. Lucey; Lieutenants—J. A. McMartin, J. L. Hughes; First Sergeant, W. D. Bessey; Quartermaster-Sergeant, W. L. Thompson; Sergeants—G. M. Francis, J. W. Gray, J. Milliken, J. Alexander; Corporals—W. C. Measure, A. J. Pettidider, J. T. Mulligan, A. Snyder, R. Fairchild, J. Sherburn; Musicians—L. M. Pollard, J. A. Griffin; Privates—M. Adams, O. J. Addison, Bert Anderson, F. W. Arnold, E. R. Barfoot, D. E. Barney, D. L. H. Bennett, C. H. Bilderbeck, J. J. Byrne, P. T. Casey, G. E. Coe, R. A. Connor, B. D. Conrad, A. D. Cook, C. C. Crever, J. Crowley, J. T. Curtis, T. Davenport, A. C. Davis, T. M. Denton, R. T. Dixon, R. T. Dunton, O. M. Faulkner, A. W. Fisher, J. Fricke, Howard Goslin, H. Gray, F. Gunter, F. H. Gwinn, B. T. Hancock, Homer Hapeman, D. O. Hilderbrandt, H. Heintz, G. W. Hodge, C. Harrigan, J. H. Johnson, A. T. Jones, E. T. Kellogg, J. W. Leslie, C. Lusie, W. B. Ludlow, C. A. Martin, J. B. McCarthy, J. C. McNairne, C. Moone, H. A. Moynahan, J. A. Mulligan, F. S. O'Brien, M. J. Olea, Charles Redman, F. D. Ryan, Charles J. Schultz, G. W. Scott, F. Silvera, H. T. Smith, W. O. Smith, C. H. Steigler, E. P. Stoddard, E. Stover, Thomas M. Strahn, T. J. Temple, T. J. Torpey, E. T. White, William L Woodman, A. Ward, H. Y. Zink, H. Zumwalt.

COMPANY G—BAKERSFIELD—

Captain, W. H. Cook; Lieutenants—Lucian Beer, B. A. Hayden; Sergeants—K. C. Masteller, J. T. Dimbleby, C. E. Harding, H. J. Haley, F. J. Downey, C. L. Dunn; Corporals—J. G. Broom, C. R. Blodget, F. H. Stanley, W. J. Reddy, G. D. Zeh, John Pennington; Musicians—L. E. Moon, C. W. Kirk; Privates—A. H. Abrams, J. C. Ashby, C. W. Ballinger, H. Barclay, I. Barnes, W. Barnes, J. Barnes, William Barnhart, J. L. Benoit, F. F. Blackington, Earl Bodley, H. H. Boren, D. E. Brewer, A. A. Brunty, A. M. Cammack, E. W. Chandler, C. M. Colton, W. T. Colton, A. S. Colton, E. R. Crane, A. S. Crites, G. S. Crites, F. W. Crocker, L. A Cunningham, J. R. Daly, T. E. Davis, B. L. Dinwiddie, Eugene Dixon, R. Durnall, A. R. Elder, D. Fielder, G. N. Fraser, R. E. L. Garner, W. G. Garrison, Charles Gorby, Fred Hamilton, W. G. Hewitt, F. M. Hicks, E. A. Hicks, W. T. Hunt, L. A. Ice, G. C. Ingles, W. H. Kelso, F. J. Kincaid, A. Kunkelman, O. C. Lindgren, G. O. Manley, John Manning, F. H. Mills, E. T. Munsey, H. P. McKenzie, W. Olds, C. H. Ortte, J. H. Paulk, W. H. Powers, E. J. Ruddy, John Savage, A. R.

Shurtleff, Jesse Timson, I. W. Tucker, S. P. Walser, J. B. Ware, G. W. West, A. T. Whittam, H. C. Winter.

COMPANY H—MERCED—

Captain, A. S. Guthrie; First Lieutenant, R. Vandenheuval; Second Lieutennt, A. R. Newell; Sergeants—J. L. Harper, T. L. Bearwald, Milo Bingam, H. Gosner, L. E. Berry, James Barbour; Corporals—W. G. Marshall, I. O. Christie, L. A. Hooper, J. W. Kelly, H. C. Seymour, J. H. Eaton; Musicians—M. Pospishek, H. Y. Law; Privates—C. C. Bettencourte, W. Casad, B. F. Griffith, G. M. Hollidge, J. A. Johnson, M. H. Keegan, C. R. Shaffer, J. E. H. Siehs, L. R. Steele, A. W. Anderson, R. Atherton, C. C. Barfield, C. F. Bartlett, F. Baumbach, C. Brandt, N. Bruce, J. M. Collins, L. O. W. Culbertson, W. E. Dalton, F. Dodson, W. C. C. Eggleston, G. S. Estey, G. W. Farrar, W. D. Farrar, J. B. George, J. Greenwood, H. H. Hail, P. Hansen, J. C. Harrington, L. Hawlett, N. Isnor, C. W. Lewis, J. A. Lewis, J. McCann, M. McLaughlin, G. B. McNeill, G. Mason, J. F. Mitchell, J. G. Mull, G. E. Myers, W. F. Neundorff, W. Nolan, R. Nunenmaker, M. L. Pease, W. G. Raitt, V. J. Sage, L. B. Silvey, W. Stern, J. F. Stockman, J. E. Traxler, J. Wagenbauer, E. A. Walters, W. H. Wegner, A. M. Wheeler, G. A. Williams, S. H. Wills, A. E. Wood, F. P. Yates, F. R. Michel, H. M. Burke, W. J. Ford, J. W. Higgins, E. G. Lonergan, F. Paul, W. Rusch, R. W. Sicafoose, F. Wickenhauser.

SEVENTH REGIMENT.

John R. Berry	Colonel Commanding
William G. Schreiber	Lieutenant-Colonel
Frank C. Prescott	Major
Dana R. Weller	Major
William O. Welch	Major
Herbert D. Alfonso	Captain and Adjutant
Amos W. Kimball	First Lieutenant and Quartermaster
James J. Choate	Major and Surgeon
William C. Roblee	Captain and Surgeon
Philip W. Russell	Captain and Surgeon
Ira C. Ladd	Captain and Assistant Surgeon
H. E. Higbey	First Lieutenant and Battalion Adjutant
John D. Frederick	First Lieutenant and Battalion Adjutant
Charles P. Fenner	First Lieutenant and Battalion Adjutant
Alfred S. Clark	Captain and Chaplain
Raymond S. Follmer	Sergeant-Major
John E. Sullivan	Quartermaster Sergeant
Paul Heydenreich	Principal Musician
Robert Burns	Principal Musician
Edward G. Bradley	Chief Musician
Arnott L. Marsh	Hospital Steward
Ira A. Allen	Hospital Steward
James M. Lothrop	Hospital Steward

BAND—Jesse Fountain, John C. Jacques, Joseph J. Jones, Grove Ketchum, F. E. Malone, M. F. Pierce, A. L. Randall, George H. Spencer, Claude Woolman, R. W. Whitney, Thomas B. Weed.

A CHRONICLE OF THE WAR.

COMPANY A—LOS ANGELES—

Captain, R. Wankowski; First Lieutenant, H. A. Bates; Second Lieutenant, A. W. Bradbury; First Sergeant; H. C. Miles. Sergeants—R. McReynolds, A. S. Clark, George O. Lockwood, Frank D. Shearer, L. C. Wells; Corporals—J. C. Specht, J. Macmillan, L. E. Foster, H. G. French, S. L. Holt, George E. Austin; Musicians—F. L. Schueddig, Frank J. Beaver; Privates—L. C. Dalton, C. Elezalda, E. P. Goetz, E. A. Johnson, L. T. Johnson, O. I. Lockwood, L. T. McKee, C. H. W. Pratt, F. C. Prescott, Jr., G. A. Reeves, G. C. Rhein, F. F. Asken, J. C. Barr, Charles T. Bradshaw, James Breen, Miles S. Brown, A. J. Bruce, Max Brust, Charles T. Bullard, H. C. Chapin, D. B. Camp, Brett Clark, John D. Cornell, M. M. Dalton, Roy Davis, Burt Dermitt, Richard Desmond, A. C. DeMotte, C. I. Eaton, L. H. Eaton, B. C. Evans, R. S. Garrett, C. M. Goor, C. M. Harrick, W. H. Holt, E. M. Hopper, I. L. Isaacs, John W. Kohane, A. M. Klein, Joseph Laventhal, George A. Law, Earl R. Lorance, W. H. Lyon, George F. Mead, William R. Morrison, C. I. MacReynolds, Charles Millan, Joseph Robbins, A. J. Russ, Charles E. Shular, C. G. Searle, H. L. Smith, Joe L. Smith, William H. Taylor, C. L. Thomson, D. T. Thompson, F. U. Velzy, I. E. White, H. C. Wilson, R. M. Galbreth, H. C. Hodgson, T. L. Krebs, John M. Maquone, Clemens Schmitz, Carl J. Christensen.

COMPANY B—SAN DIEGO—

Captain, R. V. Dodge; Lieutenants—J. C. Mielke, George T. Lemon; Sergeants—H. S. Johnstone, C. E. Chase, John M. Smith, F. A. Heilbron, Alvin E. Wright; Corporals—E. A. Lavin, Charles B. Ogden, E. H. Donn, R.C. Byers, A. M. Pullman, John M. Loop; Musicians—Leroy Arnold, H. L. Griffith; Artificer—George H. Horden; Wagoner—George R. Minter; Privates—F. A. Gillen H. E. Krause, J. O. Lapp, W. A. Traver, F. W. Tupper, Chas. M. Bryan, Herbert Beckwith, Frank E. Barbour, F. E. Chapman, E. E. Cox, F. H. Catherwood, D. B. Dodson, W. T. Drury, John E. Ellis, W. M. Farmer, F. Gillespie, E. F. Golding, N. Hansen, C. S. Hall, H. C. Israel, F. Johnson, N. A. Jolls, J. R. Kingston, Frank Lee, J. N. Maddox, R. B. Miller, F. A. Mailander, H. R. Marshall, O. D. Marshall, William J. Miller, M. M. Moulton, C. A. McDermouth, C. F. McNealy, James F. McCleary, G. J. McKenzie, Andy J. McCollen, Robert D. McClain, George E. Conaughy, George W. Noble, H. L. Parsons, C. E. Plaisance, Edward Powers, D. D. Ranch, A. E. Roberts, R. O. Rude, John P. Russell, D. G. Sampson, James B. Scott, Roy Stowell, James E. Swycaffer, W. M. Thompson, E. E. Thompson, D. A. Thompson, Jose Villa, A. D. Worden, John W. Wheeler, Jr., John Warren, P. E. Woods, Emil Dobler, William Harvey, C. C. Overshiner, George P. Sikes, C. T. Tichborne, George Warner.

COMPANY C—LOS ANGELES—

Captain, S. T. Langworthy; Lieutenants—F. Cole, James A. Holden; Sergeants—A. C. F. Dee, W. H. Courtney, F. W. Hall, A. R. Story, Charles H. Brown; Corporals—G. F. Wonnersley, A. G. Coulson, James E. Hill, Charles S. Church, James E. F. Aiken, H. O. Preston; Musicians—Charles Lehn, Ray W. Scott; Artificer—William B. Higgins; Wagoner—George B. Dunn; Privates—L. Allenson, C. J. Baker, J. H. Burke, D. P. Bottroff, B. G. Cleveland, J. S. Davidson, W. Davis, Jr., G. Fisher, A. R. Hazeltine, A. Kohler, F. J. Pollock, W. S. Prine, W. H. Schueddig, T. B. Scott, F. H. Smith, George E. Aull, R. W. Avery

E. N. Baker, A. A. Berryman, S. E. Britton, C. R. Bryant, William H. Carter, E. G. Chadsey, Charles B. Christy, Ben R. Clark, William J. Clark, Homer L. Cole, Ross Cummings, Lee L. Davis, William Dodge, Jr., William Gill, A. J. Grant, O. W. Hann, L. N. Huff, W. W. Ingraham, F. J. Kupper, S. B. Krutz, William B. Laughn, George Lidgerwood, Jr., Alva L. McDonald, Charles S. McEwen, John J. Miller, P. Meissen, Prelen A. Molmark, Frank Nightwine, C. E. Pomeroy, Leander Quint, Bert Rees, Albert Reinschild, Roy Rogers, Bert Roes, E. F. Schulz, James B. Scott, Charles E. Sheppard, George W. Simpson, Raymond M. Smith, Charles R. Story, E. G. Thomas, Oteo Thomas, R. O. Whiteside, H. G. Whitlock, Charles G. Wilmon, Jr., C. H. Wood, F. C. Woodward, G. C. Davidson.

COMPANY D—POMONA—

Captain, Harry T. Matthews; Lieutenants—John A. Eason, Samuel Crawford; Sergeants—E. F. Schoch, Charles E. Dudley, Alba M. Hurtt, Leon F. Beckett, Charles F. Spencer; Corporals—O. A. Charlton, Chauncey M. Baughman, Thomas E. Mills, John R. Crapo, Elera J. Meud; Privates—D. Andrews, H. N. Barnes, F. J. Baker, C. F. Bowen, C. B. Brown, W. Charlton, G. C. Day, C. A. Johnson, L. W. Heath, Milo S. Bowen, Sam Butler, Hugh A. Broaded, Horace Bickford, N. J. Bishop, A. A. Carter, E. V. Caldwell, J. B. Cashon, George W. Dorr, Oakar F. Ek, Harry E. Fromyer, G. A. Gaylord, John G. Gibson, Charles W. Harris, B. Hawkins, H. F. Kerwig, John H. Hill, E. H. Keller, H. E. Lane, John Linstruth, Clarence P. Longwell, Carlyle E. Latta, Maurice E. Ludden, C. F. Lichtenwalter, Roy Miner, O. B. Manchester, William F. McKennon, B. McKennon, A. R. Newcomb, T. E. O'Neill, C. M. Peters, M. J. Pierce, E. C. Patton, G. D. Percival, Henry Roberts, F. E. Rothaermel, J. A. Rightmier, A. L. Stone, C. R. Staples, John A. Simmons, Ezra Snoke, W. Tom Scott, F. A. Snook, C. P. Talbert, C. E. Underwood, E. C. Wright, C. P. White, Fred Moody, B. L. Wells, F. E. Wilson, O. E. Watson, H. E. Ward, David Wanner, George W. Yarrow, C. B. Young, Carl Ziegler, P. A. Burnett, Charles H. Hinton, Charles McLachlan, William E. Stevens, Earl B. Wallace.

COMPANY E—

Captain, Charles H. Fernand; Lieutenants—O. G. Kenney; John I. McKenna; Sergeants—Ruy E. Moore, George H. Skinner, O. J. Hardison, Ray Mitchell, Charles E. Bell, Frederick W. Cole; Corporals—James F. Rolls, James H. Rogers, Charles M. Sackett, W. T. Steele, Z. G. Graham, William L. Hagenbaugh; Musicians—H. A. Burrows, William F. Davis; Privates—G. S. Allen, Jr., F. W. Allen, H. F. Bandy, F. W. Bradley, Charles F. Benn, Alex Bell, F. O. Boughn, M. Barnett, Aug. Beard, Frank Beard, William D. Blair, LeRoy Confer, D. N. Cummings, W. L. Cook, J. J. Daly, Charles W. Davidson, A. L. De Nure, Charles O. Dewey, J. J. Dunn, E. M. Frankland, George Ferguson, George W. Farrell, O. L. Freeman, John H. Glazebrook, M. J. Hill, R. W. Hickok, E. W. Hobbs, C. F. Hewett, George P. Hanna, A. R. House, James H. Jeffs, F. M. Kelsey, F. W. Lloyd, Charles M. Logan, E. S. Logsdon, George H. Lattemore, James R. McKell, R. E. Mahan, William Mullen, Guy McGhee, James M. Morris, R. J. Newman, John L. Pound, Henry Pruitt, Charles N. Puckett, H. W. Perkins, A. O. Roseveare, T. E. Rosenberg, C. R. Rice, F. G. Russell, F. H. Danborn, O. V. Sprague, C. M. Stone, M. G. Seeley, I. E. Smith,

A CHRONICLE OF THE WAR. 151

Nathan Sharp, T. G. Shafer, R. S. Torrey, G. Thurmond, L. C. Weisbach, Fred Williams, Orry S. White, A. H. Wilder, H. L. Williams.

COMPANY F—LOS ANGELES—

Captain, F. L. Reynolds; First Lieutenant, J. A. Winans; Second Lieutenant, J. A. Wymans; Sergeants—G. Ferguson, W. A. Wing, H. E. Culver, Frank Harlan, T. O. H. Bogalsky, Roy C. Prentiss; Corporals—R. M. Conley, L. E. Meyer, L. P. Neitz, K. E. Tomlinson, Canby Hewitt, Benjamin C. Robinson; Musicians—George Bacon, S. J. Van Buskirk; Privates—N. D. Bennett, P. D. Caulkins, L. A. Florentin, H. Johnson, G. S. Lockwood, R. W. Lewis, F. H. McGuire, J. R. Powers, J. T. Price, F. L. Anderson, William Benson, Edward J. Borgmeyer, Robert E. L. Bryan, William Brennier, F. C. Bledsoe, H. H. Capell, R. G. Corbin, C. E. Chappelear, J. J. Chaney, Leopold De Los Rios, C. A. Dalton, John H. Drew, H. L. Dunton, Frank J. Earl, Leonard Fox, Charles Freedman, Charles E. Fisk, Clinton C. Finley, Edward Gibson, Speed C. Guyer, H. L. Hathaway, Hugo Mathias, Hans H. Hemb, E. P. Keogh, W. E. King, S. L. Kems, H. H. Morgan, C. A. Miller, F. H. McQuaid, T. J. McMullin, U. G. Neff, A. E. L. Neitzke, F. L. Pugh, T. J. Roessen, F. L. Reade, M. C. Rissinger, E. G. Stiles, A. J. Swift, John Sheerer, Sam Solomon, C. F. Samuelson, William S. Tuthill, John W. Winder, Melvin Young, Allen W. Benjamin, William H. Ball, E. S. Bany, William S. Deets, H. K. Perdew, C. J. Stone, Jr.

COMPANY G—REDLANDS—

Captain, George S. Biggin; First Lieutenant, George M. Smallwood; Second Lieutenant, Lewis Palmtag; Sergeants—G. E. Cryer, H. F. H. Brown, L. K. Brown, Frank Cook, James E. Hoskig, Jacob Kircher; Corporals—E. S. Logie, W. H. Fletcher, Charles Ford; A. G. Reynolds, O. H. Burton, James F. Earl; Musicians—Wilbert R. Sisson, Charles Danielson; Privates—J. G. Baldridge, A. W. Hunt, C. J. Johnson, E. B. Lukens, F. J. Michaelis, C. L. Rucher, J. A. Mack, Jr., John H. Toll, Joseph Allen, William E. Arnold, William W. Bender, Peter Brooks, Albert C. Brown, A. P. A. Brown, George J. Butler, Frank F. Corbin, George C. Cousins, F. W. Cryer, Oliver Cummins, Frank Curless, S. P. Derbyshire, Frank S. Dicks, Peter Dickie, William W. Dixon, Charles E. Foster, Henry A. Fowler, P. B. Greason, James M. Gwin, Lemuel B. Gwin, Hugh C. Gwynn, Clifford Heidt, H. S. Hinckley, N. B. Irons, John S. Kindcher, Clarence B. Kline, George W. Knapp, M. J. Lewis, Cornelius Lyman, Archie MacGrady, William Marske, August Millard, H. J. McCormick, Thomas J. O'Brien, John O'Dea, William K. Pettit, Frank C. Preston, Adam Reising, B. L. Roberts, W. H. Ross, A. J. Rhodes, N. C. Scott, A. C. Sheppard, A. C. Sherman, M. D. Sherrard, M. E. Shorey, Jr., Frank Thomas, William D. Tuirmonds, Charles F. Tilden, Frank J. Valdez, George A. Weber, George A. Willet, Jr., Oscar V. Williams, Eugene W. Woodbury, L. J. Wood.

COMPANY H—VENTURA—

Captain, A. W. Browne; Lieutenants—John W. Hammons, James R. Daly; Sergeants—J. C. Larmer, F. C. Hunt, George W. Johnson, Leroy C. Bates, Samuel P. Rowe, George H. Baker; Corporals—Jesse C. Joy, Charles E. Huston, Charles A. Gondolfo, C. P. Eastin, John Hund, J. M. Waterman; Musician—A. O'B. Browne; Privates—Frank

Blackstock, Lester W. Bernheim, John C. Barnard, William S. Bell, Harman Corey, H. W. Churchman, George L. Daly, J. O. Dockery, Dennis P. Hickey, William Illenstein, Harry Hunt, Oliver T. Jones, William A. Larison, Thomas McGuire, John R. Orton, Frank I. Rodibaugh, Albert Swasey, George G. Arnold, Frank Butler, M. M. Collins, E. T. Carter, John W. Clark, George H. Cuplin, Robert Craig, Joseph S. Donaldson, Fred L. Danford, William Eagon, Oscar Fish, Martin Fitch, John A. Fake, Harry P. Flint, Henry C. Foltz, Thomas Friend, James R. Fraser, C. H. Gillespie, William Hamilton, William W. Hunter, M. C. Hobart, Cephas Jones, William A. Larison, S. Lorenzano, L. H. LeValley, H. Lehme, James M. Mikesell, H. G. Masgrove, Martin Maher, Victor Mungari, W. H. Martin, John Mitchell, William H. Marcelaine, Thomas O'Donnell, R. W. Pidduck, A. J. Reynolds, William A. Rowland, F. H. Rodibaugh, George R. Reynolds, Gabriel Ruiz, A. L. Russell, R. H. Staples, William C. Smith, Charles R. Sheldon, Rea W. Smith, Charles A. Tripp, Sam W. Tyson, Harry E. Wilson, John D. Wiltfong, Thomas Wilden.

COMPANY I—PASADENA—

Captain, W. L. Lippencott; Lieutenants—F. B. Thayer, Harry La V. Twining; Sergeants—W. S. Keyler, J. A. Griggs, E. I. Packard, H. E. Stibbens, L. D. Collins; Corporals—A. C. Jones, E. G. Weil, J. E. Colston, F. E. Billhuner, Frank H. Nixon, F. H. Burtt; Musicians—F. R. Jones, Charles A. Findley; Privates—F. G. Cooper, J. L. de Groot, William G. Allen, James H. Buchanan, Charles F. Buchanan, George W. Banbury, M. S. Banbury, Joseph E. Barrett, A. P. Bartholomy, George A. Batchelder, N. H. Cox, W. Copping, Thomas D. Davis, J. H. E. Everett, P. G. Garlick, Charles W. Greene, H. F. Gentry, I. J. Hobart, H. E. Kuntzman, William E. King, E. F. Kooper, Louie W. Lange, Claude Laytham, Charles D. McKee, George Metz, Samuel A. McCormick, R. McManaman, J. P. Osborn, George W. Perviance, James F. Presnall, James L. Pettigrew, Charles R. Poole, R. H. Reed, L. J. Packard, S. J. Reed, H. G. Sutton, John Sprague, David F. Swift, H. M. Stowe, A. B. Slater, Arthur J. Santong, George E. Smith, S. C. Sleet, W. B. Shaver, William H. Thrall, A. A. Thompson, Charles H. Yocum, W. A. Douglass, Lawrence O. Thornburgh, I. S. Adams, A. H. Bandel, Paul D. Green, H. H. Galtman, Oscar S. Kunzman, Warren P. Michener, F. J. McGowan, L. G. Regnier, Harry L. Schofield, F. L. Clark.

COMPANY K—SAN BERNARDINO—

Captain, Orin P. Sloat; Lieutenants—W. S. Seccombe, Arthur F. Holpin; Sergeants—H. J. White, W. G. Bodkin, C. S. Rollins, John D. Matthews, William A. Roundtree, Byron W. Allen, Donald W. Strong; Corporals—D. L. Noble, A. J. Rodgers, Frederick J. Atkinson, Joseph P. Doyle, A. B. Gazzola, Joseph L. Whitlock; Musicians—D. S. Brown, C. A. King; Privates—John W. Averill, Frank Baker, Edwin L. Barrows; Sherman G. Bachelor, William T. Baxter, Charles E. Binckley, Arthur Brill, Ned N. Brown, E. I. Cleveland, Leroy A. Coburn, J. I. Cole, Paul B. Conant, W. S. Cooper, C. C. Corkhill, Riland Cox, Andrew Craig, John E. Crain, Charles E. Crawford, W. R. Davies, H. G. Davis, E. L. Davis, James P. Dolan, William H. Dubbs, Starkey Duncan, Albert D. Frantz, Rudolph A. Fremlin, Reuben B. Glaze, Cuthbert Gully, John Hall, George W. Hendley, James Hospelhorn, B. L. Houck, V. T. Johnson, Arden H. Kellar, Edwin La Niece, William LeRue, George E. Lanterborn, John A. Magill, J. B. Mann, Ira S.

Martin, L. E. Mitchell, Thomas G. Mort, Charles K. McDonald, Robert Nelson, Charles H. Nicholson, H. N. Peck, George G. Osborn, R. C. Powell, John Purcell, William H. Ralston, Charles Reat, F. W. Singer, Jr., K. E. Smith, J. W. Stollicker, George W. Swing, Theodore H. Tarbox, Emery B. Tyler, William F. U. Ren, Arthur Walton, Joseph C. Wever, John Weil, Lemuel G. White, George E. Whitlock, William B. Williamson, Joseph L. Worley, John W. Young, Nicholas Young.

COMPANY L—SANTA ANA—

Captain, Solomon H. Finley; Lieutenants—Walter A. Greenleaf, Lewis L. Vestal; Quartermaster Sergeant, A. F. Smith; Sergeants—George Magill, L. R. Brock, John C. Abbey, Charles W. Hannah, Louis A. Barrett; Corporals—W. B. Bowers, B. E. Johnson, Clyde L. Bishop, Earl G. Glenn, Emerson Collier, Francis L. Weber; Privates —C. Adams, E. F. Barton, L. Carmack, M. C. Cooper, H. A. Chase, H. M. Day, W. Dunham, D. D. Field, H. F. Higley, C. Kepley, R. F. Vegeley, V. E. Zerman, Leonidas H. Adams, James A. Austin, Charles W. Barker, Charles E. Bowman, David Bush, Leroy L. Chandler, Emery A. Clough, Thomas Y. Dilley, William A. Eades, Gary M. Field, James Farmer, Birney H. Fisk, Guy W. Holladay, James S. Hatfield, Edwin C. Hickey, Wiel Higgins, Frank C. Hosler, Clinton Imes, Thomas B. Johnson, E. N. Kuizenga, Oscar S. Kurtz, John Love, Fred W. Lutz, Benjamin F. Lutz, Perry B. Lyon, Linton E. Manuel, John O. McGougan, William L. McDivitt, Charles W. McNaught, Bert C. McMurray, Thomas M. McReynolds, Joseph Mefford, Charles A. Winter, Arthur Newman, Warner P. Nail, N. H. Northcross, Robert Northcross, Everett F. Ogborn, Clifton J. Overshiner, William Renner, Albert H. Sitton, Samuel Shannon, W. C. Smith, A. R. Stedman, G. E. Talbot, Charles A. Turner, Harry G. Upham, Charles E. Waffle, Alof H. Warling, E. R. Bradbury, William P. Northcross, Gilbert Campbell, Edward Evans.

COMPANY M—RIVERSIDE—

Captain, Charles F. Pann; First Lieutenant, H. J. Bedwell; Lieutenant, Charles B. Bayley; Sergeants—Harry E. Mitchell, John T. Short, John W. Horton, William E. Thompson, Edward R. Nicholson, Foy D. Battle; Corporals—C. J. Baldwin, D. F. Bell, G. B. Cox, E. A. Meacham, Francis M. Horton; Musicians—Goss Bernard, Edwin A. Merwin; Privates—S. M. Bloom, P. J. Bollinger, L. J. Burnham, C. A. Cover, W. D. Craig, W. Evans, B. F. Fairchild, A. D. Gage, H. F. Nelson, W. P. Pann, C. W. Rohrer, H. T. Harr, William T. Babcock, Frederick E. Barney, William H. Brunacombe, Dennis A. Ball, Charles B. Beldin, Hunter Bowen, Arthur D. Bell, John G. Bryan, George H. Campbell, Herbert S. Cunningham, Louis Craig, Judd C. Cleveland, Forest R. Cleveland, Thomas H. Dix, Cornelius Donaghue, Edgar Gardener, Herman Gessler, Edward Grant, Harry E. Goodrich, Henry Haskell, Myler M. Harris, Eddie A. Hart, Joseph R. Hamer, Scott LaRue, Rodger T. Labadie, Alex Law, David A. Moriarty, Warren J. Marsh, Robert V. Meyer, Edward H. Mercer, Eddie W. Mort, Otis H. Mort, Eugene C. Johnson, Clarence C. Jarvis, Jacob Jacobson, Daniel A. Newcomb, George E. Pomeroy, Floyd Pomeroy, John H. Petterson, William H. Painter, John W. Reck, Samuel H. Ralph, Walter R. Strong, George Scott, James J. Schultz, George D. Taylor, Harry Tobias, Joseph N. Thornton, Jesse Van Meter, John M. Young, Frederick Kniss, Philip N. Van Slyck, James J. Cook, Fenn D. Twogood, Ralph L. Ditto.

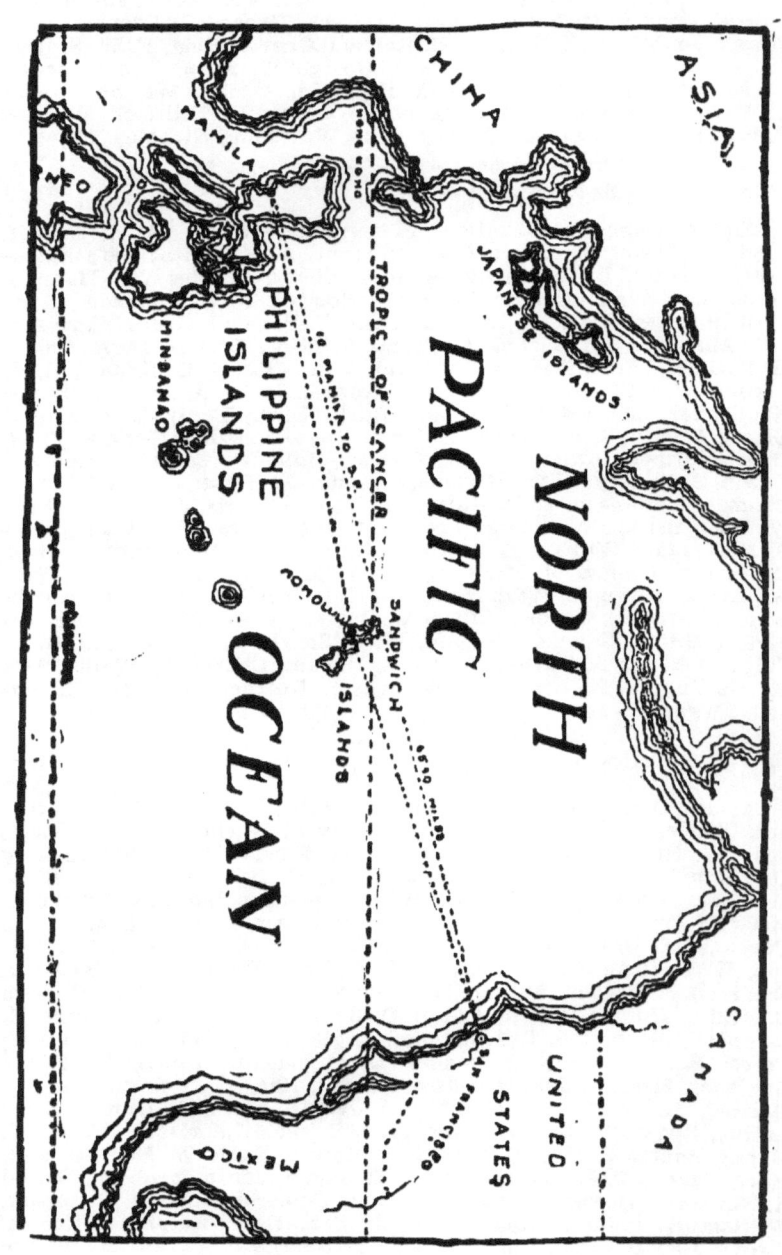

LOCATION AND DISTANCES OF THE PHILIPPINES.

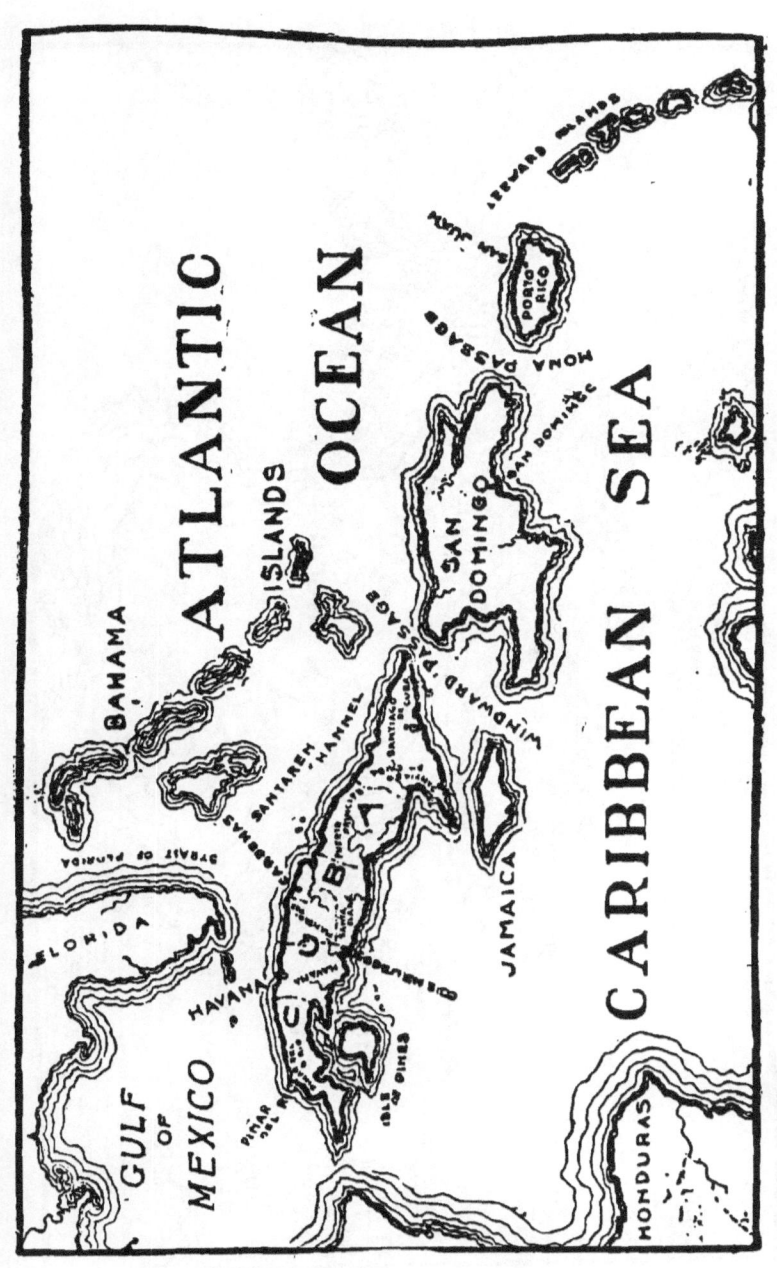

CUBA AND THE WEST INDIES.

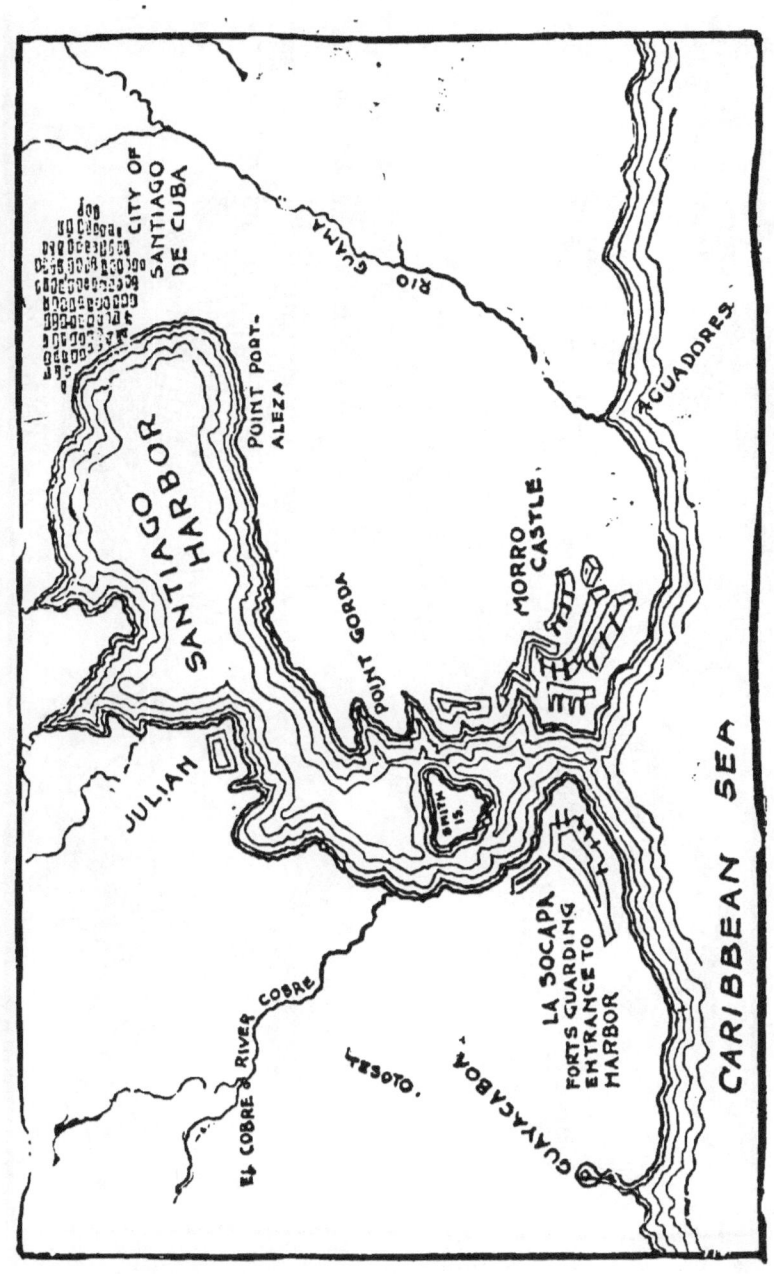

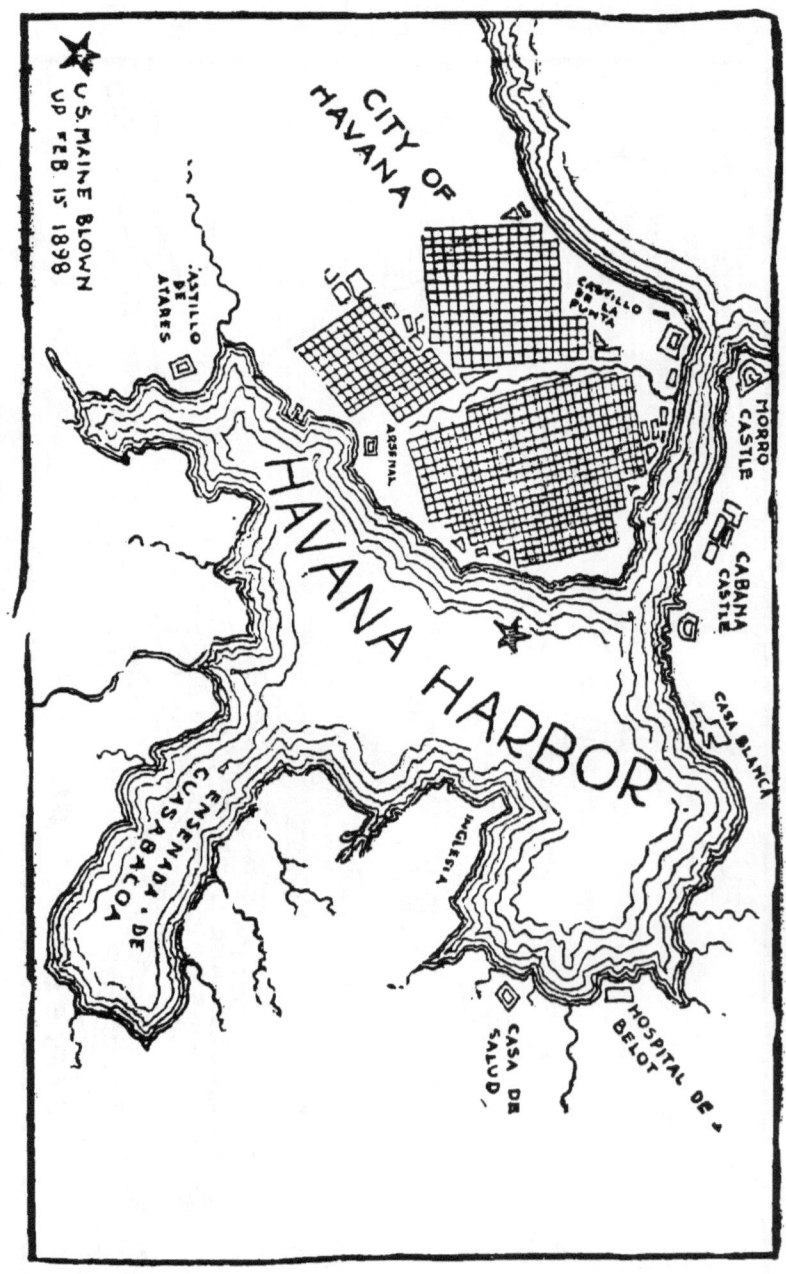

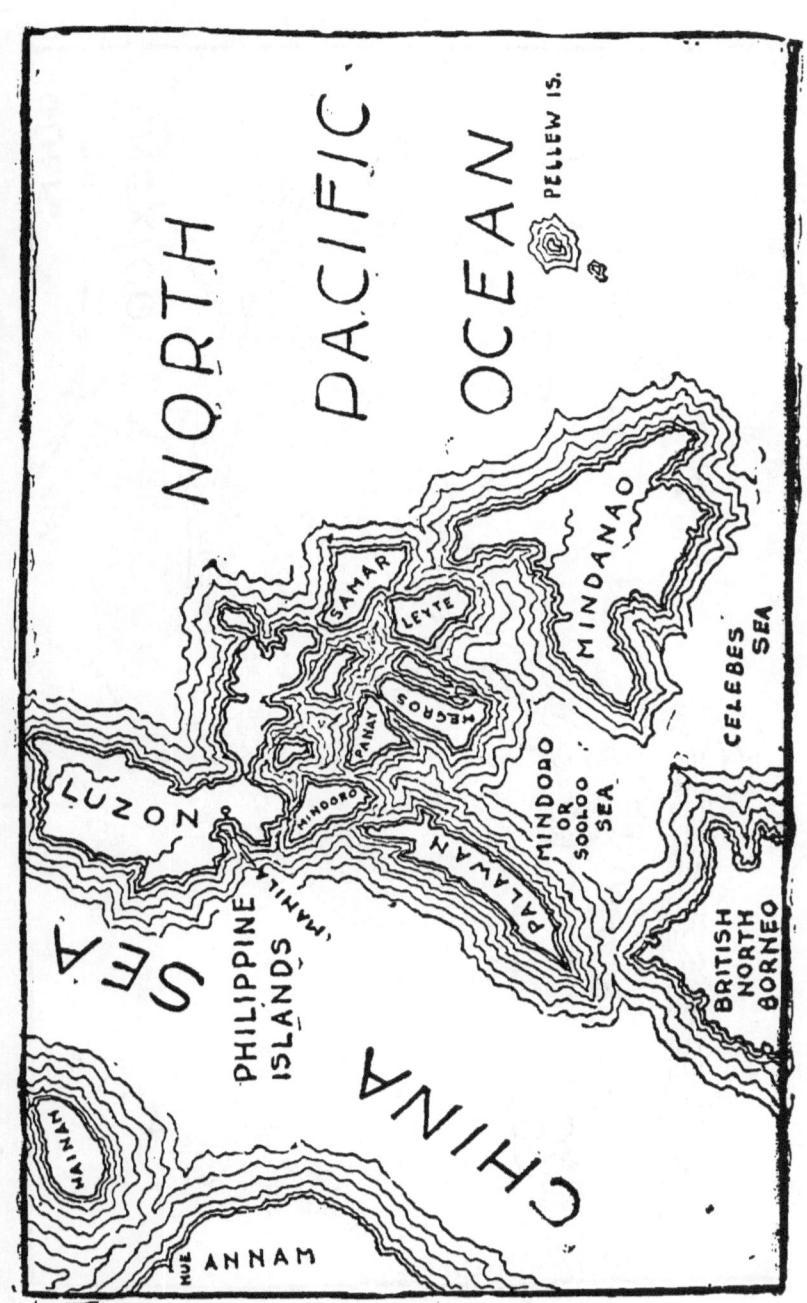

THE PHILIPPINE ISLANDS.

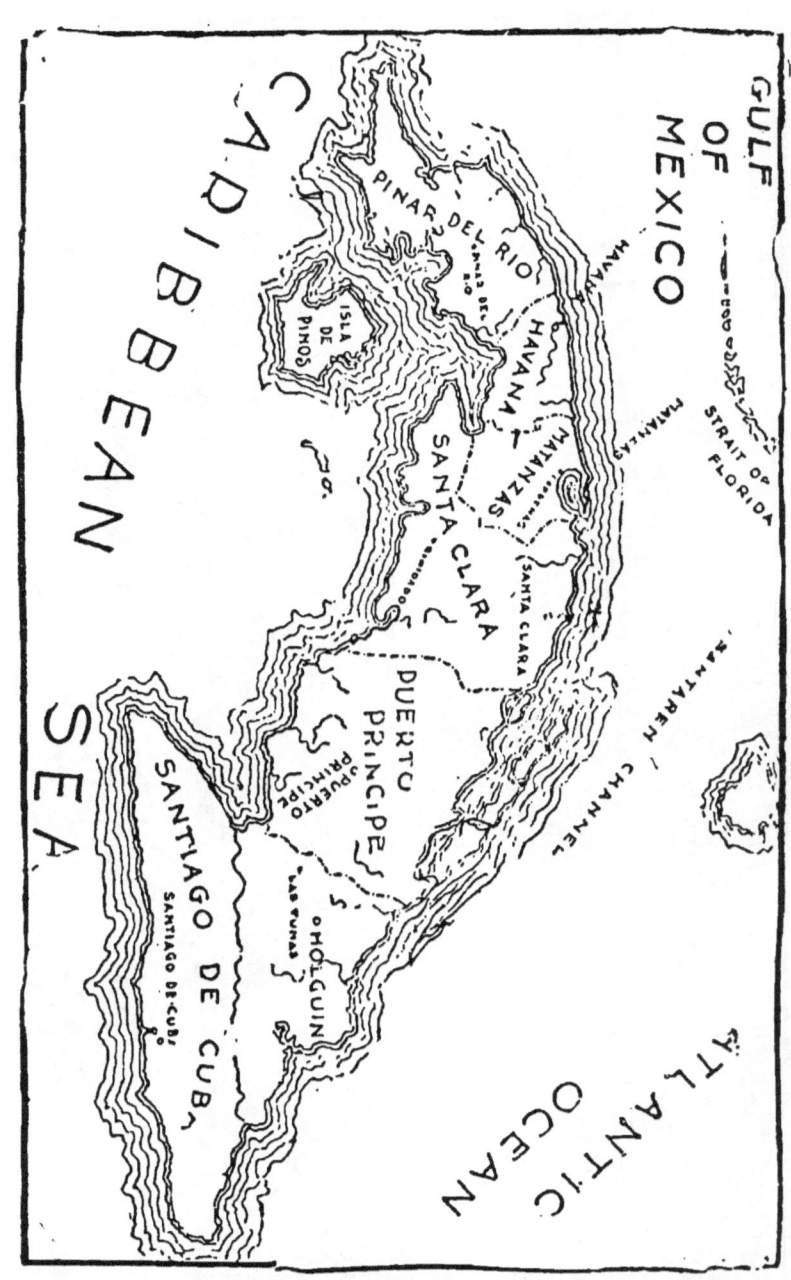

MAP OF CUBA.

WAR   WAR   WAR

NEWS

Subscribe for

THE BULLETIN

And you will get all the News of the War

14 HOURS IN ADVANCE

Of the publication of the same news in the Morning Papers of San Francisco

❧ ❧ ❧

50 Cents a Month
BY MAIL OR CARRIER

❧ ❧ ❧

ADDRESS

THE BULLETIN
San Francisco, Cal.

The San Francisco BULLETIN
Prints the News 14 hours in advance of Morning Papers

www.ingramcontent.com/pod-product-compliance
Lightning Source LLC
Chambersburg PA
CBHW030254170426
43202CB00009B/733